The pursuit of form: a study
of Hawthorne and the romance

The pursuit of form: a study of Hawthorne and the romance

by

John Caldwell Stubbs

(1970)

University of Illinois Press

Urbana Chicago London

© 1970
by the Board of Trustees of the University of Illinois
Manufactured in the United States of America
Library of Congress Catalog Card No. 70-104025
252 00097 8

To June

Contents

Introduction

When a critic addresses himself to a writer of the stature of Nathaniel Hawthorne, one of his prime concerns must be what makes this writer unique. He must ask what resides in the writer's work to make it last where other contemporary works have not lasted and what stamps it distinctly recognizable as the work of one man different from all others who have written. The answer for Hawthorne, I feel, is not so much in the subjects he treats, nor in the various attitudes he takes toward these subjects; it is not in his understanding of the psychological complexity of his characters; and it is not in his use of language. All of these elements are very important to Hawthorne's success. They have been well treated by previous critics, and quite rightly so. But they do not constitute the essence of Hawthorne's fiction. This essence, the stamp that makes his work Hawthornian, resides in his sense of form.

My assertion will not come as a thunderclap of revelation for most readers and critics of Hawthorne. Much of the scholarship of the past two decades is predicated on the notion that form is extremely important in Hawthorne's work. Certainly, this is the main thrust of Richard Harter Fogle's *Hawthorne's Fiction: The Light and the Dark* and Hyatt H. Waggoner's *Hawthorne: A Critical Study*. And Roy Male, in *Hawthorne's Tragic Vision*, while maintaining that his focus is Hawthorne's romantic view of life, actually spends much of his energy on the organizing principles in the discrete works. The only serious challenge to the idea that form is the basis of Hawthorne's greatness is Frederick C. Crews's *The Sins of the Fathers: Hawthorne's Psychological Themes*. Crews suggests that we have tended to lose sight of the considerable psychological complexity in Hawthorne's works. While he is undoubtedly correct in that assertion, I would wish to disagree with him that this psychological complexity is at the root of Hawthorne's power as an artist. Hawthorne does not offer the sprawling range or the profound depths of psychological gropings of a Dostoevski. Rather, he offers a certain amount of psychological complexity which is carefully shaped. Also I should like to disagree with Fogle, Waggoner, and Male, who, following F. O. Matthiessen's *American Renaissance*, have tended to emphasize ambiguity above all else in their discussions of form. They are correct in stating that Hawthorne's form often depends on his offering alternative interpretations to the ethical or moral dilemmas he sets. But ambiguity can be misleading. Almost always Hawthorne narrows the alternatives to a fairly compact range of balances and contrasts. Instead of asserting, for instance, that Dimmesdale, Hester, and Chillingworth all react to the fact of sin in their different ways, we might note that of all the possible ways of reacting to sin Hawthorne has reduced his view to a consideration of three.

What I am pointing to, then, is the idea that Hawthorne exerts much more control over his material than most critics are willing to admit and that his quite self-conscious shaping and the resulting lucidity are not detriments but rather the sources of his strength.

We should recognize that literature has always involved a conflict between the artist's urge to reproduce human experience in its rich diversity and his antithetical urge to structure and confine the experience in order to communicate something about it. At different points in history and to different writers one pole will seem more important than the other. Clearly for Wyatt, Surrey, and the Elizabethan sonneteers the structuring and the expression of an experience were more important than the experience itslf. For naturalists Zola, Dreiser, and Farrell, the rawness of the material was to spill out as directly as possible. The French symbolists, if we follow Northrop Frye's remarks about them in *The Anatomy of Criticism*, push this attitude to the extreme. Their poems are not modifications of experiences; they *are* the experiences unreduced. (Only the puckish will ask how these men acquired experience in metrics.)

Certainly in the twentieth century, we look to the pole of rich diversity with a strong bias. Tolstoi is a greater writer than Chekhov, we tend to say, because he encompasses so much more of life. It follows that we should rediscover Melville and see him eclipsing Hawthorne, because he ranges so much further. Conversely when we move to defend our liking for Hawthorne, we often do so in terms of the variation he is able to capture on his small scale. We defend his art as we defend the art of a deadpan comedian. The fact that the latter freezes his cheek muscles makes his eyes more expressive. Whatever this says of deadpan comedians, it is nonsense when applied to Hawthorne. It is an example of criticism supplying bad reasons for good responses, as T. S. Eliot would have it. Hawthorne's merit is a positive one. It is his ability to streamline human experience to exactly the right point where it retains some feel of human diversity, psychological complexity, and moral ambiguity, but more importantly, overridingly, gives the reader a sense of these things ordered in a very precise work of art.

In a sense, Hawthorne was lucky to have been born when he was, for he fell heir to a literary theory which suited him exactly, the theory of the romance. This theory provided him with guidelines for highly structured works of art. Hawthorne accepted these guidelines and worked to realize their possibilities. Each of his four major works involves experimentation with the given materials of the romance.

Two men, Richard Chase and Northrop Frye, have examined the form of the romance at some length. Chase, in *The American Novel and Its Tradition*, approaches the romance in order to prove a point about later novels. He wants to show that the American realistic novel grew from the romance and took on, therefore, a bolder, wider scope than the English novel, which was derived from the more constrained tradition of realism beginning with Defoe. "Nothing will be gained by trying to define 'novel' and 'romance' too closely," he states. But the romance, he feels, may be summarized in capsule form as follows: "the romance, following distantly the medieval example, feels free to render reality in less volume and detail. It tends to prefer action to character, and action will be freer in a romance than in a novel, encountering, as it were, less resistance from reality." If this were indeed a true definition of the romance, we would do well to wonder why Hawthorne insisted he was a writer of romances, for this definition has little to do with the kind of fiction Hawthorne created. But the definition will not hold up. It is Chase's invention. Much more to the point is Chase's argument that the characters and their relationships are "somewhat abstract and ideal," with the result that "the romance will more freely veer toward mythic, allegorical, and symbolistic forms." This is correct, and it is a useful point of entry into Hawthorne's fiction. But we need to realize that this kind of "veering" is toward artifice and structure, not toward the kind of expansiveness Chase would have us believe is the root substance of the prose romance.

Northrop Frye, in *The Anatomy of Criticism*, is a more acute critic. He looks at the romance as a critical "mode" which cuts across historical periods. This allows him to see Hawthorne's *The*

Marble Faun in the context of the Arthurian fables. He defines the romance by means of the abilities of the characters: "If superior in *degree* to other men and to his environment, the hero is the typical hero of *romance*, whose actions are marvellous but who is himself identified as a human being. The hero of romance moves in a world in which the ordinary laws of nature are slightly suspended: prodigies of courage and endurance, unnatural to us, are natural to him, and enchanted weapons, talking animals, terrifying ogres and witches, and talismans of miraculous power violate no rule of probability once the postulates of romance have been established." The area of romance exists between the realm of gods in myth and the realm of human beings in realism.

Frye and, to a certain extent, Chase point us in the right direction. They both suggest a fictional world of the romance which is somehow different and removed from the world we function in. But I would suggest that we can be much more specific on how nineteenth-century writers created that world and why they claimed to have created it. When we examine the essays, introductions, and critical reviews on the form of the romance, side by side with the romances themselves, we will uncover a consistent, reasonably elaborate theory of fiction. Hawthorne's own pronouncements on the romance, as we shall see, derive from this nineteenth-century body of critical material. I propose in this book to set about clarifying nineteenth-century notions of the romance and then go on to consider how Hawthorne uses them in creating his own distinctive forms.

While tracing the ideas on the form of the romance, I shall be moving somewhat counter to another, better-known nineteenth-century conception—the idea of "organic" form. As Emerson spells it out in "The Poet" and his journal, this idea gives primacy to experience and inspiration over "mechanical" craftsmanship. The experience will suggest or evolve its own form. Such an attitude, while it may be important to certain nineteenth-century Romantics, seems to have little to do with Hawthorne's art. To put it bluntly, Hawthorne cares about "mechanical" craftsmanship; he cares very much. Unless the idea of "organic" form is reduced considerably from Emersonian hyperbole to the point where it means only molding form to meaning, the idea does stand opposed to the body of critical attitudes surrounding the romance. The body of attitudes I will be tracing puts heavy emphasis on problems of "mechanics." It is concerned with artifice.

In my first chapter, I define the romance in the terms of nineteenth-century writers and critics and show how Hawthorne assimilated the parts of their definition, sometimes straightforwardly and sometimes ironically. The romancer aimed at creating a fictional world set at a distance from ordinary experience, and he pursued this distance by working with three groups of antitheses. We can see examples of this distance in typical nineteenth-century romances about Puritanism and revenge. Hawthorne used the assumptions of romance theory, and he even used some of the conventional situations of nineteenth-century romances, but he, more than the other writers, was prepared to emphasize the highly contrived artifice of the romance form. Rather than trying to thrust the reader directly into simulated human experience, Hawthorne attempted to confront him with the process of the artist self-consciously probing and ordering human experience. Through artifice, Hawthorne sought to make us conscious of the drama of the mind searching for meaning in fiction.

I treat Hawthorne's tales from two points of view in my second chapter. First, I consider "The Artist of the Beautiful" and "Rappaccini's Daughter" as illustrations of the drama of the artist's mind as he weighs one set of possibilities against another. Second, I examine Hawthorne's metaphor of the individual and the "procession of life" in order to understand better the kind of affirmation of the human condition Hawthorne wishes his characters to make. "My Kinsman, Major Molineux," "Young Goodman Brown," "The Canterbury Pilgrims," and "The Maypole of Merry Mount" are the tales I treat at length. This analysis of the tales concludes the first part of the book, designed to establish approaches to Hawthorne's romances.

Part Two contains chapters on *The Scarlet Letter*, *The House of the Seven Gables*, *The Blithedale Romance*, and *The Marble*

Faun. With *The Scarlet Letter*, I concentrate on the conflict of the "black Puritan" and the "fair Puritan" as Hawthorne's means to limit and structure his examination of man's place in the sin-stricken human condition. In *The House of the Seven Gables*, my main concern is Hawthorne's artifice of setting up a comic world with one set of characters only to parody and criticize it with another set. The irony of Hawthorne's creating a series of tragic struggles for power and showing them through the eyes of a comic, powerless narrator is the source of the artifice I consider in *The Blithedale Romance*. With *The Marble Faun*, I concern myself mainly with the work's dreamlike texture. It is my contention that Hawthorne gives us there a sense of the mind turning and sifting possibilities in the Adamic myth. Each of the four major romances represents a kind of experimentation with the artifice of romance distance, on the theme of the individual's need to affirm the "procession of life." In each of the four we are made very much aware of human complexity being brought into organizing form. This structuring artifice was the strength inherent in the romance form that Hawthorne was able, uniquely, to realize.

My debts are large. No one can write on Hawthorne today without borrowing more than he adds to scholarship. In particular I have used heavily the works of Fogle, Waggoner, Male, and Crews. I wish to thank Professors Willard Thorp and Richard Ludwig, who helped me early in the preparation of this study, and Edward Davidson, whose thoughtful readings have aided me in the final preparation of the manuscript. And I wish to thank those of my students who were willing to hear me out on Hawthorne and exchange ideas with me.

Portions of Chapters I and III of this book have appeared previously in *PMLA*, and sections of Chapter VI in the *Emerson Society Quarterly*. I would like to thank the editors of both journals for granting me permission to use this material again in new form.

Part one

Perspectives

Chapter I

<hr>

Hawthorne
and the form of the romance:
a historical view

Nathaniel Hawthorne was the master of the form of the American romance. It is as craftsman, as "pure" writer, that he stands out in the development of American literature. He adopted his literary theory and even some of his fictional materials from contemporary writers and therefore was able to direct his creative energies mainly toward shaping the theory and the materials into carefully textured artifice.[1] During the 1840's, Hawthorne's "apprentice pe-

---

1 Several modern scholars have treated aspects of the romance in America. Probably the best known is Richard Chase, *The American Novel and Its Tradition* (New York, 1957). Since his aim is to show how the novel

3

riod" before he wrote his four major long works, the romance became accepted gradually by American authors and readers as a
form with its own distinct set of aims and rules. Prior to that time,
although writers as well known as Charles Brockden Brown and
James Fenimore Cooper had discussed it, the word *romance* was
so closely linked with the idea of frivolity that American writers
seldom used it in their titles as a generic term. During the 1840's,
however, the term came under serious scrutiny, and the genre was
recognized as valid.[2] Beginning with *The Scarlet Letter*, subtitled
"a romance" and published in 1850 when the term was well established, Hawthorne asked explicitly that his long fiction be judged
according to the aims of the genre.[3] He declared himself a romancer.

grew from the romance, however, he does little more than pull together some major statements by Cooper, Simms, and Hawthorne before
moving on to develop this thesis. More interesting is Joel Porte, *The
Romance in America* (Middletown, Conn., 1969), which treats the
theme of exploration of the wilderness, either geographical or psychological, in the works of Cooper, Poe, Hawthorne, Melville, and James,
but Porte does not occupy himself much with the *form* of the romance.
My main debts in this chapter are to the following historical studies of
nineteenth-century romance theory: G. Harrison Orians, "The Romance
Ferment after Waverley," *American Literature*, III (January, 1932), 408–
431; William Charvat, "Fiction," *The Origins of American Critical
Thought: 1810–1835* (Philadelphia, 1936), pp. 134–163; and Alexander
Cowie, Introduction, *The Yemassee by William Gilmore Simms* (New
York, 1937), pp. ix–xxxv. These scholars have pointed out the increasing
number of reviews and critical prefaces about the form in the first part
of the 1800's.
2 In Lyle Wright's *American Fiction, 1774–1850* (San Marino, Calif., 1948),
only twenty-two works entitled romances are recorded as published before 1840, but for the period 1840–45, forty are listed, and for the period
1846–50, seventy-one.
3 Hawthorne's awareness of contemporary romances is so well known
that it scarcely needs rehearsal here. He was well read in the works of
Scott, the Gothic romancers, and Cooper, and in the critical journals of
his time. In addition we may note remarks made by his sister Elizabeth
that he read popular books from the circulating library. (See Julian
Hawthorne, *Nathaniel Hawthorne and His Wife* [Boston, 1884], I, 125,
and Randall Stewart, *Nathaniel Hawthorne: A Biography* [New Haven,
1948], p. 27, and "Recollections of Hawthorne by His Sister Elizabeth,"

The primary aim of the romancer is to gain an artistic distance from human experience. The romance differs from the novel in the extent of this distance. The English romancer Sir Walter Scott, in "An Essay on Romance," distinguished between the "marvellous and uncommon incidents" in the romance and the "events ... accommodated to the ordinary train of human events" in the novel,[4] and the American romancer William Gilmore Simms, in *The Yemassee*, between the "possibility" of a situation in the romance and the "probability" of a situation in the novel.[5] Both were following essentially the definition laid out by the English Gothic romancer Clara Reeve in her dramatized essay *The Progress of Romance* (1785): "The Romance is an heroic fable, which treats of fabulous persons and things.—The Novel is a picture of real life and manners and of the times in which it is written. The Romance in lofty and elevated language, describes what never happened nor is likely to happen.—The Novel gives a familiar relation of such things as pass every day before our eyes. ..."[6] Precisely in this vein is Hawthorne's famous distinction between the novel and the romance in the Preface to *The House of the Seven Gables*. It is Hawthorne's most explicit statement that he wants to put his fictional world at the artistic distance of romance.

American Literature, XVI [January, 1945], 324.) This is not to assert that Hawthorne read romances uncritically, however. He was clearly distressed that romancers used historical subjects often as a means to platitudes about American life. This concern is bluntly put in his 1846 review of William Gilmore Simms's *Views and Reviews*, where he dismisses the historical themes and eras championed by Simms for the American romance on the grounds that they would have to be "cast in the same worn out mould that has been in use these thirty years." (Quoted in Randall Stewart, "Hawthorne's Contributions to the *Salem Advertiser*," *American Literature*, V [January, 1934], 331.) Hawthorne was as conscious of facile and mechanical uses of romance theory as he was conscious of the potentials of the form.

4 Scott, "An Essay on Romance," *The Miscellaneous Prose Works of Sir Walter Scott, Bart.* (Edinburgh, 1827), VI, 155-156.

5 Simms, *The Yemassee. A Romance of Carolina* (New York, 1835), I, vi-vii.

6 Reeve, *The Progress of Romance and The History of Charoba, Queen of Aegypt*, ed. Esther M. McGill (New York, 1930), I, 110-111.

> When a writer calls his work a Romance, it need hardly be observed that he wishes to claim a certain latitude, both as to its fashion and material, which he would not have felt himself entitled to assume, had he professed to be writing a Novel. The letter form of composition is presumed to aim at a very minute fidelity, not merely to the possible, but to the probable and ordinary course of man's experience. The former—while, as a work of art, it must rigidly subject itself to laws, and while it sins unpardonably, so far as it may swerve aside from the truth of the human heart—has fairly a right to present that truth under circumstances, to a great extent, of the writer's own choosing or creation.[7]

This kind of distance or latitude attributed to the romance does not necessarily imply an escape from human experience. In fact, as Hawthorne's catch phrase "the truth of the human heart" suggests, the romancer's quest for distance could have a strongly pragmatic, moralistic basis. Traditionally, the romance was defended as experience structured. English apologists and critics in the eighteenth century had argued that fiction was a valuable means of instruction when a writer simplified and arranged human experience to demonstrate patterns of morality.[8] Experience abstracted in such a way is life held at a distance. Eventually it became clear that the nineteenth-century romancer's professed goal was to order the random happenings of experience into artful patterns so that the reader could *comprehend* the experience—either intellectually or emotionally. It need hardly be added that few romancers lived up to this goal. The goal existed, and it was available to Hawthorne. The romance, then, may be considered an approach to human experience, not a flight from it, yet an approach much more ordered, much more patterned, than the reader's chaotic meeting with experience in his daily life, or even in the novel.

To approach experience in such a way is, of course, to put heavy emphasis on artifice. The romancer calls attention to the process of ordering he undertakes. Such an approach was well suited to Haw-

7 Hawthorne, *The House of the Seven Gables*, Centenary Edition (Columbus, 1965), p. 1.
8 See, e.g., James Beattie, "On Fable and Romance," *Dissertations Moral and Critical* (London, 1783), pp. 505–506, and Reeve, *The Progress of Romance*, II, 86–87.

thorne's particular cast of mind. Emerson, though he erred in com-
plaining, was right in his basic observation when he commented
that Hawthorne "invites his readers too much into his study, opens
the process before them. As if the confectioner should say to his
customers, 'Now, let us make a cake.' " Hawthorne may well have
been one of the most self-conscious writers ever to seize a pen. He
was as much interested in the *process* of analyzing human experience as he was in the experience itself. Better than any other romancer he was able to take advantage of the artificial nature of the
romance. He used the romance distance self-consciously as a means
to make the reader aware that he was seeing experience in the process of being abstracted and comprehended. In other words, Hawthorne used romance distance as a means to engage the reader in a
debate about human experience. More often than not in his tales
and always in his long romances, Hawthorne represented experience as subject matter for dialectical inspection. Rather than providing answers and rarely providing *ambiguity* (the term most
often used for Hawthorne's complex works), Hawthorne provided different voices for a dialectic process. The distance of the
romance gave Hawthorne a form in which he could experiment
with and develop the self-conscious use of artifice. This distance
was enormously important to him.

In order to achieve the proper kind of distance, the romancers
discussed and used, without actually codifying, three interrelated
balances: verisimilitude and ideality; the natural and the marvelous; and history and fiction. We shall trace briefly here the historical development of attitudes about these balances and examine
some examples of romances published during Hawthorne's "ap-
prenticeship" which claimed to use these balances, in order to see
the theory and the kinds of stylized situations he drew on and converted to a high order of self-conscious artifice.

The balance of verisimilitude and ideality is, of course, basic to
most theories of fiction. The romancer, however, was especially
concerned with the delicateness of the balance. By the words *ideality* and *ideal* he meant conceptual abstraction. An abstract pat-

tern of meaning was to be balanced with the appearance of reality. To be sure, *ideality* and *ideal* had certain philosophical connotations in nineteenth-century culture. The German post-Kantian idealists Fichte, Schelling, and Hegel—popularized in the English-speaking world by the Romantics and the Transcendentalists—used *ideal* to describe self-thinking Thought or self-creating Spirit that to them was existence. Hegel, in particular, saw art as a fusion of the ideal with sensuous form and considered the fusion a step toward the perception of existence.[9] In America, Emerson duplicated this attitude. The Emersonian poet was defined as a sayer who expressed his intuitive perception of the Spirit. Emerson told the poet: ". . . the ideal shall be real to thee." [10] At the same time, there continued in England and America an eighteenth-century, neo-classic notion in art and literature of portraying the ideal, in the sense of the general type, of concretions in the natural world. This was the critical principle of Sir Joshua Reynolds in his third discourse when he described the artist's method: "His eye being enabled to distinguish the accidental deficiencies, excrescences, and deformities of things, from their general figures, he makes out an abstract idea of their forms more perfect than any one original; and what may seem a paradox, he learns to design naturally by drawing his figures unlike to any one object. This idea of the perfect state of nature, which the Artist calls Ideal Beauty, is the great leading principle by which works of genius are constructed." [11] Reynolds' theory of art is mimetic, whereas the theory of Emerson is expressive. But few romancers distinguished. More important to them was the fact that both theories involved the interplay

9 I have in mind here one of Hegel's main theses in his lectures on art first published in German in his collected works in 1835. The lectures were not translated into English until 1920. Because this is so, I do not insist on Hegel as a direct influence on American romancers. Rather, I consider him a good representative of German idealism, which generally influenced English and American thinkers. See G. W. F. Hegel, *The Philosophy of Fine Art*, trans. F. P. B. Osmaston (London, 1920), 4 vols.

10 Emerson, "The Poet," *The Complete Works of Ralph Waldo Emerson* (Boston, 1903), III, 42.

11 Reynolds, "Discourse III," *The Works of Sir Joshua Reynolds* (London, 1797), I, 39–40.

of real life with conceptual abstraction. Whether a romancer saw the interplay as mechanical or organic, he knew his craft depended on the solution of the balance.

At first, American critics insisted that all writers of fiction should strive mainly for verisimilitude in order to make their works ineluctably relevant to human experience. Typical of this position is the declaration of the American reviewer for the *Port Folio* in 1816: "The novelist should copy real life as nearly as possible; ideal scenes and characters, however suited to the dignity of poetry, are incompatible with that diversity of incident, and alternative of manner, which constitute the life and spirit of every performance, which professes to exhibit the miscellaneous volume of human life." [12] The reviewer deals with all fictionalists, making no distinction between romancer and novelist, and urges them to copy real life in detail. Just such an attitude is also maintained by self-proclaimed romancer Marshall Tufts, who, in his Introduction to *Shores of Vespucci; or Romance without Fiction* (1835), claimed his book was the first "genuine" romance on the grounds that "not a single fictitious sentence is knowingly allowed in it." [13]

Yet, also from the first, other romancers mocked the principle of verisimilitude as an end in itself. In a jocular dialogue prefacing a romance on the War of 1812, Samuel Woodworth wrote: " 'The absurdity of the incidents must not be imputed to me,' said I, 'they are all copied from life.' " [14] The point he wishes to make through irony is, I take it, that the writer of fiction must assume responsibility for ordering the events in his work. He must admit he is the arranger in his fictional creation. Responsibility does, indeed, fall on the author.

The point is made more forcefully and more elaborately by Edward Bulwer-Lytton, the prolific English author of both ro-

---

12 *Port Folio*, Fourth Series, II (August, 1816), 161.
13 Tufts, *Shores of Vespucci; or Romance without Fiction* (Lexington, Ky., 1833), p. 3.
14 Woodworth, *The Champions of Freedom, or The Mysterious Chief, A Romance of the Nineteenth Century, Founded on the Events of the War, between the United States and Great Britain Which Terminated in March 1815* (New York, 1816), p. iv.

mances and novels, in his essay "The Critic." Using the analogy
of sculpture, Bulwer-Lytton insists on the importance of the artist's ability to find ideal or abstract configurations in his subject
matter and the relative triviality of the skill necessary to reproduce
his subject matter in mechanical detail. For Bulwer-Lytton, both
execution and *conception* determine the excellence of a work of
art. But of the two, the conception, which he defines as the artist's
grasp of an ideal or abstract pattern, is the more important. Conception should determine the execution of the work, not imitation
of nature: "For the Ideal consists not in the imitation, but the ex-
alting of Nature; and we must accordingly inquire, not how far it
resembles what we have seen so much as how far it embodies what
we can imagine." [15] His essay is a defense of the ideal over the real.
And following his line of reasoning to its conclusion when he turns
to a consideration of the romances of Walter Scott, Bulwer-
Lytton is forced to attack his acknowledged mentor for too much
emphasis on verisimilitude and not enough on abstract design.

    In America, James Fenimore Cooper was in close agreement
with Bulwer-Lytton's critical position. After a decade of fame,
Cooper spoke his mind freely in his 1832 Introduction to *The
Pioneers:* "As this work professes, in its titlepage, to be a descriptive tale, they who will take the trouble to read it may be glad to
know how much of its contents is literal fact, and how much is
intended to represent a general picture. The Author is very sensible that, had he confined himself to the latter, always the most
effective, as it is the most valuable mode of conveying knowledge
of this nature, he would have made a better book." [16] He, too,
argues for the importance of a "general picture" over the repro-
duction of literal fact. And certainly the abstract values of reason
and intuition represented by various characters in his Leather-
stocking Tales serve to put Cooper's works on the level of moral

15 Bulwer-Lytton, "The Critic," *Monthly Chronicle*, I (March, 1838), 43.
16 Cooper, *The Pioneers, or The Sources of the Susquehanna; A Descrip-
    tive Tale* (London, 1832), I, v. Cf. *The Pioneers* (New York, 1823), I,
    viii–x. In the first-edition Preface Cooper had discussed the need to curb
    imaginative flight, but by 1832 he was sufficiently established to volte-
    face and defy the American critical emphasis on fidelity to fact.

generalization. Cooper and Bulwer-Lytton, assuredly, were opposed by the majority of early nineteenth-century critics in America who feared (often correctly) that any variation from the appearance of reality would lead to escapist literature. Nevertheless,
Bulwer-Lytton and Cooper were powerful literary figures. Their
endorsement of idealization and abstraction helped to adjust the
critical temper and set clear what tendencies must be balanced in
the romance.

Hawthorne followed the balance exactly. One of his major ef-
forts as a romancer was to blend his idealized patterns of meaning
with the appearance of reality to achieve the artistic distance of
romance. In his tale, "Drowne's Wooden Image," the praise the
artist Copley gives to Drowne's work is put in romance terms: "It
is as ideal as an antique statue, and yet as real as any lovely woman
whom one meets at a fireside or in the street." [17] Hawthorne
wanted this same balance in his own work, and his constant worry,
as no critic has failed to remark, was that his fiction lacked verisimilitude.[18] His self-criticism in the introductory statement to

17 *The Complete Works of Nathaniel Hawthorne*, Riverside Edition
(Boston, 1883), II, 354. Hereafter this edition will be cited as *Works*.
18 Hawthorne's self-pronouncements and his literary theory have received
serious attention only within the last twenty-five years, but in that time
span they have received attention with a vengeance. Virtually his every
remark on fiction has been tabulated in one or more of the following
essays: Charles Howell Foster, "Hawthorne's Literary Theory," *PMLA*,
LVII (March, 1942), 241–254; Roy Harvey Pearce, "Hawthorne and the
Twilight of Romance," *Yale Review*, XXXVII (Spring, 1948), 487–506;
Jessie Bier, "Hawthorne on the Romance," *Modern Philology*, LIII
(August, 1955), 17–24; Harry Hayden Clark, "Hawthorne's Literary and
Aesthetic Doctrines as Embodied in His Tales," *Transactions of the
Wisconsin Academy of Sciences, Arts, and Letters*, L (1961), 251–275;
Robert Kimbrough, "'The Actual and the Imaginary': Hawthorne's
Concept of Art in Theory and Practice," *ibid.*, pp. 277–293; Richard
Jacobson, *Hawthorne's Conception of the Creative Process* (Cambridge,
Mass., 1965); and Mary Rohrberger, "Hawthorne's Literary Theory and
the Nature of His Short Stories," *Studies in Short Fiction*, III (Fall,
1965), 23–30. Despite this large amount of work, we have yet to understand Hawthorne's basic emphases clearly. This is because most of the
critics above view Hawthorne as an isolated aesthetician. Nothing could
be further from the truth. Most of his pronouncements are part of a
continuing dialogue in American letters on the nature of the romance.

"Rappaccini's Daughter" shows his fear that his work has only "the faintest possible counterfeit of real life," and in the Preface to *The Twice-Told Tales* he regrets that his stories have "the pale tint of flowers that blossomed in too retired a shade." Equally as well known as these self-judgments is his admiration for writers like Trollope who were far more realistic than he. But from a different standpoint, in his description of Dr. Johnson's Uttoxeter in *Our Old Home* we find Hawthorne offering a very different argument. Because in the past he had idealized Dr. Johnson's penance in Uttoxeter into a scene of great power, when he came to the actual spot where the penance took place, Hawthorne was shocked to find the scene different from his conception of it. The disparity between the ideal and the real provoked him to think further on the relationship of the two and to comment, indirectly, on the artistic process of the romancer:

> A sensible man had better not let himself be betrayed into these attempts to realize the things which he has dreamed about, and which, when they cease to be purely ideal in his mind, will have lost the truest of their truth, the loftiest and profoundest part of their power over his sympathies. Facts, as we really find them, whatever poetry they may involve, are covered with a stony excrescence of prose, resembling the crust on a beautiful sea-shell, and they never show their most delicate and divinest colors until we shall have dissolved away their grosser actualities by steeping them long in a powerful menstruum of thought. And seeking to actualize them again, we do but renew the crust. If this were otherwise,—if the moral sublimity of a great fact depended in any degree on its garb of external circumstances, things which change and decay,—it could not itself be immortal and ubiquitous, and only a brief point of time and a little neighborhood would be spiritually nourished by its grandeur and beauty.[19]

Hawthorne's point is that the ideal truth of the scene of penance is more valid than the externals of the spot. His idealization is the "fact," and Uttoxeter only the "crust" around it. Hawthorne is not talking of subjective truth; he is talking of discovering and

---

The context of this dialogue serves to clarify many of Hawthorne's remarks about his art.

19 *Works*, VII, 165–166.

picturing scenes of universal truth. His notion is platonic and, here at least, Transcendental. We find similar probing in "The Old Manse" when Hawthorne asks whether reflections seen in the Concord River are symbols of a higher reality: "Which, after all, was the most real—the picture, or the original?—the objects palpable to our grosser senses, or their apotheosis in the stream beneath?" [20] His search for an ideal truth or an abstract, universal pattern beneath the surface of reality, tentative as it always is, suggests that his concern with verisimilitude in fiction has to be seen in a larger frame of reference than is usually the case.

Aesthetically, Hawthorne is clear enough about the relationship of the ideal and the real. The two are to be balanced. His worry about realism is no more than worry that one side of the balance is out of kilter. An image of perfect balance is Miriam's studio in *The Marble Faun:* "The room had the customary aspect of a painter's studio; one of those delightful spots that hardly seem to belong to the actual world, but rather to the outward type of a poet's haunted imagination, where there are glimpses, sketches, and half-developed hints of beings and objects, grander and more beautiful than we can anywhere find in reality." [21] The studio is a perfect image for the balance Hawthorne desires. It mingles objects from the physical world with the fragments of abstract conceptions from the artist's "haunted imagination" literally contained in the half-worked-out sketches. The studio is midway between the physical world and the artist's mind. The room images the romancer's role to blend the two realms. Hawthorne insists on this role for himself in the prefaces to all four of his major romances. He tells us, in *The Scarlet Letter*, that he is "creating the semblance of the world out of airy matter." [22] In *The House of the Seven Gables*, he brings "his fancy-pictures almost into positive contact with the realities of the moment" (p. 3). Within the framework of *The Blithedale Romance*, "the creatures of his brain

---

20 *Works*, II, 32.
21 *The Marble Faun: or, The Romance of Monte Beni*, Centenary Edition (Columbus, 1968), p. 41.
22 *The Scarlet Letter*, Centenary Edition (Columbus, 1962), p. 37.

may play their phantasmagorical antics, without exposing them to too close a comparison with the actual events of real lives." [23] And in *The Marble Faun*, Hawthorne uses Italy as the site of his "fanciful story," because it is a "fairy precinct, where actualities would not be so terribly insisted upon" (p. 3).

His literary theory is further clarified by his metaphors of the moonlight, the mirror, and the half-dream. All three he uses over and over again. The first of these, the moonlight, is associated with the romancer's imagination. The moonlight allows us to see reality in an abstracted way. This is best developed in "The Custom-House" when Hawthorne's persona considers his fictional material in his moon-drenched chamber:

> Moonlight, in a familiar room, falling so white upon the carpet, and showing all its figures so distinctly,—making every object so minutely visible, yet so unlike a morning or noontide visibility,—is a medium the most suitable for a romance-writer to get acquainted with his illusive guests. There is the little domestic scenery of the well-known apartment; the chairs, with each its separate individuality; the centre-table, sustaining a work-basket, a volume or two, and an extinguished lamp; the sofa; the book-case; the picture on the wall;—all these details, so completely seen, are so spiritualized by the unusual light, that they seem to lose their actual substance, and become things of the intellect [p. 35].

In the moonlight the objects of the room retain the details of their daylight appearance, but they also seem to Hawthorne "spiritualized" into abstractions of the mind, "things of the intellect." The passage quoted here is used by Hawthorne to prepare the reader for the artistic distance he will encounter in *The Scarlet Letter*. Hawthorne uses his persona's movement from the substantial, everyday world of the Custom House's ground floor, to the "airy hall" of the unfinished second story of the building, to the moon-drenched chamber where he confronts the ghost of Surveyor Pue and other projections of his "haunted imagination," as a gradual and carefully contrived movement to the distance of the romance.

The second metaphor, the mirror, is perhaps more a device to

23 *The Blithedale Romance and Fanshawe*, Centenary Edition (Columbus, 1964), p. 1.

bring about an effect in Hawthorne's various works than it is a means to explain a theory. But for the moment at least, we may regard it as a metaphor. Since F. O. Matthiessen has demonstrated Hawthorne's numerous uses of the mirror,[24] it remains for us only to note, in the context of romance theory, that the mirror's surface holds a two-dimensional abstraction of a three-dimensional real object. Quite literally, the mirror's surface fuses the ideal and the real. Often Hawthorne exaggerates this effect. A good instance is Hilda's mirror in *The Marble Faun*. Because of a chance position at one point in the action, the mirror superimposes Hilda's "real" face on the portrait of Beatrice Cenci which is an "ideal" presentation of Hilda's moral situation. Similarly, in *The Scarlet Letter*, the convex mirror of Bellingham's armor holds together the real person Hester and an ideal image of her situation when it shows her covered by the letter *A*. Seen this way, Hawthorne's metaphor of the imagination as mirror, offered in "The Custom-House," is very apt indeed.

Closely related to these two metaphors is the half-dream. Hawthorne describes the state of a person half awake, half asleep in "The Haunted Mind": "You have found an intermediate space, where the business of life does not intrude; where the passing moment lingers, and becomes truly the present; a spot where Father Time, when he thinks nobody is watching him, sits down by the wayside to take breath." [25] We can accept this moment suspended within the flow of time as a metaphor for the creative state when Hawthorne's persona in "The Custom-House" describes himself before the parlor fire, in the moonlight, dreaming "strange things" and making them "look like truth." He is half in the real world of time and half in a world of the mind which seems outside time. Not surprisingly Hawthorne uses this suspended, balanced state early in each of four romances. The main action of *The House of the Seven Gables* begins with the slowly waking sensations of Hepzibah. In *The Scarlet Letter* and *The Blithedale*

24 Matthiessen, "The Imagination as Mirror," *American Renaissance* (New York, 1954), pp. 253–264.
25 *Works*, I, 344.

Romance, we move quickly to the dream states of Hester, looking over the throng from the scaffold, and Coverdale, looking at Blithedale from his window. And *The Marble Faun* starts with a view of "dreamy character" from the Capitol in Rome. Thus, again and again Hawthorne uses metaphors that show the balance of opposites of real objects and conceptual abstractions of the mind.

The romancer's primary goal in this balance is, as we have said, to organize experience into comprehensible form at a distance where the reader may see the form clearly. But to many nineteenth-century romancers this goal meant little more than reducing human experience to moral platitude. It became a standard ploy of romancers to announce at the start of their works the set of virtues or vices the work would illustrate. The declarations were mechanical, often little more than a hoax. Typically, Benjamin Barker, at the beginning of *The Gold Hunters . . . A Romance of the Sea*, piously intoned, "In the following romance, as in all which I have had the honor of submitting to your perusal, we have endeavored to inculcate a good and sound moral," [26] announced his work was a sermon against avarice, and then proceeded to bring forth a series of sensational crimes and abductions on shipboard, having little or nothing to do with the announced vice. Hawthorne's response to this kind of mechanical declaration was the proper one: irony.

In the Preface to *The House of the Seven Gables*, Hawthorne draws attention to his own sincere moral purpose by mocking the romancer's device of announcing his "moral." First, Hawthorne declares he must have a moral in order not to be inferior to other writers, and so he "lifts" Horace Walpole's famous biblical warning from *The Castle of Otranto:* "The sins of fathers are visited on their children to the third and fourth generation." But he undercuts the seriousness of the moral by the use of the whimsical word "mischief" and by the amusingly over-elaborate working of the metaphor of an avalanche. Hawthorne writes:

26 Barker, Introduction, *The Gold Hunters . . . A Romance of the Sea* (Boston, 1846), n. p.

Many writers lay very great stress upon some definite moral purpose, at which they profess to aim their works. Not to be deficient,
in this particular, the Author has provided himself with a moral;—
the truth, namely, that the wrong-doing of one generation lives into
the successive ones, and, divesting itself of every temporary advantage, becomes a pure and uncontrollable mischief;—and he would
feel it a singular gratification, if this Romance might effectually convince mankind (or, indeed, any one man) of the folly of tumbling
down an avalanche of ill-gotten gold, or real estate, on the heads of
an unfortunate posterity, thereby to maim and crush them...
[p. 2].[27]

His irony establishing his freedom from the mechanical process of
naming the work's moral, Hawthorne can go on to discuss seriously the moral purpose in the romance form.

When romances do really teach anything, or produce any effective
operation, it is usually through a far more subtle process than the
ostensible one. The Author has considered it hardly worth his while,
therefore, relentlessly to impale the story with its moral, as with an
iron rod—or rather, as by sticking a pin through a butterfly—thus at
once depriving it of life, and causing it to stiffen in an ungainly and
unnatural attitude. A high truth, indeed, fairly, finely, and skillfully
wrought out, brightening at every step, and crowning the final development of a work of fiction, may add an artistic glory, but is
never any truer, and seldom any more evident, at the last page than
at the first [pp. 2–3].

Hawthorne makes the point that moral truth, when illustrated in a
romance, is inherent in the subject matter and the romancer's man-
ifested attitude toward it. In the terminology of romance dicta,
we could say the moral truth is inherent in the work's ideal pattern. Hawthorne's metaphor of the butterfly should not be pushed
too far. He does not intend to equate his romance with a beautiful
but useless creation like Owen Warland's butterfly in "The Artist
of the Beautiful." In the context of this Preface, the butterfly rep-

27 Hawthorne's statement that "he would feel it a singular gratification
if . . ." is a parody of Barker's kind of declaration: "If we have succeeded,
or should succeed in any of our writings to cause any one to shudder
at, and shun the numerous vices which we have endeavored to dress in
their appropriate garbs, our great object and aim will have been accomplished, and we shall finally retire from the field" (*ibid.*, n. p.).

resents the imaginative aspects of the romance which are destroyed if the work is reduced to a simple formula of illustrating a moral.

Even in his early tales, Hawthorne approached the question of moral purpose in fiction with irony. In "Night Sketches under an Umbrella" in 1838, Hawthorne has his speaker seize on a passing stranger to supply a necessary moral for the tale: "This figure shall supply me with a moral, wherewith, for lack of a more appropriate one, I may wind up my sketch," [28] and, in his introductory statement to "Wakefield" in 1835, he invites the reader to wander with him through the tale, "trusting that there will be a pervading spirit and a moral, even should we fail to find them, done up neatly, and condensed into the final sentence." [29] Exactly the same ironic attitude carries over to his last finished romance, *The Marble Faun*, in 1860. In the Preface Hawthorne admits only, "The author proposed to himself merely to write a fanciful story, evolving a thoughtful moral" (pp. 2–3). The key word is *evolving*, which implies a developing pattern rather than a succinct moral. Within the romance itself, Kenyon tries to sum up the "moral" of Donatello's sin, but Hilda will accept neither of the solutions he offers. It is not so much that we should think Kenyon wrong; it is rather that we should see he is not *definitively* right. Hawthorne refuses to condense his romance to a single statement. In the Conclusion added to the second edition, he overtly mocks the readers who would solve the romance's moral complexity with an axiom. To them he says only that Miriam is still "at large," since she broke no law, and that Donatello is in prison, since he did. A legal answer for simplistic moralists. Hawthorne will not offer the axiom in *The Marble Faun*.

On the other hand, when he does offer it in *The Scarlet Letter* and *The Blithedale Romance*, he is so outrageously glib that his irony is obvious. Near the end of *The Scarlet Letter*, Hawthorne in his role as speculating editor gives a message worthy only of

28 *Works*, I, 484. Cf. Arlin Turner, *Hawthorne: An Introduction and Interpretation* (New York, 1961), p. 53. Turner points out that the moral of the tale has nothing to do with the tale itself.
29 *Works*, I, 154.

Polonius: "Be true! Be true! Be true! Show freely to the world, if not your worst, yet some trait whereby the worst may be inferred!" (p. 260). At the end of *The Blithedale Romance*, Coverdale, who too often tends to think along the lines of a Polonius, puffs forth: "Philanthropy . . . is perilous to the individual, whose ruling passion, in one exclusive channel, it thus becomes. It ruins, or is fearfully apt to ruin, the heart; the rich juices of which God never meant should be pressed violently out, and distilled into alcoholic liquor, by an unnatural process; but should render life sweet, bland, and gently beneficent, and insensibly influence other hearts and other lives to the same blessed end" (p. 243). The first is parody, and the second is bombast. Hawthorne is playing with the romance convention. To find the moral thrust of Hawthorne's works, the reader must follow the abstract or "ideal" pattern, worked out in the work as a whole and balanced against a semblance of the complexities of real experience.

More particular to the romance than to other kinds of literature is the interplay of the marvelous and the natural. We may trace this balance as far back as the seventeenth-century French romances of Madeleine de Scudéry who, in *Clelia* (translated, 1655), has a character argue for a fiction "which shall be at the same time marvelous and natural." But toward the end of the eighteenth century, the idea received a good deal more prominence from the English Gothic romancers Horace Walpole and Clara Reeve. Walpole explains in his Preface to the second edition of *The Castle of Otranto* that he has made his characters react in a natural way to the supernatural events of his tale, and Reeve elaborates, in her Address to the Reader in *The Champion of Virtue*, on Walpole's intentions: *The Castle of Otranto*, she claims, "is an attempt to unite the various graces of the ancient romance and modern Novel.—to attain this end, there is required a sufficient degree of the marvellous to excite the attention.—enough of the manners of real life, to give an air of probability to the work. . . ."[30]
This balance was picked up in the nineteenth century by Walter

30 Reeve, *The Champion of Virtue. A Gothic Story* (London, 1777), p. iv.

Scott and Edward Bulwer-Lytton, who offered certain refine-
ments. Scott ruled that supernatural occurrences should be used
sparingly and presented mainly through suggestive images rather
than tangible detail.[31] Marvelous actions, he urged, should not be
merely ornamental; they should contribute directly to mood and
plot. Such, he insisted, was the intended function of the supernatural action of his critically attacked White Lady in *The Monastery*.[32] Bulwer-Lytton reasoned that if a man's life has a "spiritual
level" which includes belief in the supernatural and in superstit-
tions, then the romancer who would treat this man in his entirety
must use those elements.[33] But at the same time, he felt that the
romancer must take into account the sophistication of his readers.
Historically correct supernatural beliefs which would alienate contemporary readers should be tempered by the romancer. Both
Scott and Bulwer-Lytton felt the marvelous, a source of artistic
distance, needed to be tactfully handled.

The blend of the marvelous and the natural in romance theory
was important to Hawthorne. Writing an article on John Green-
leaf Whittier's *The Supernaturalism of New England*, Hawthorne
pointed out that there was a balance of the marvelous and the natural existing inherently in New England superstitions, mainly because the New Englander's experience of settling a harsh land gave
his Old World superstitions, as Hawthorne put it, "a more sordid,
grimy, and material aspect." [34] As a romancer, he wished to nur-
ture this balance. He made this clear in his declaration at the beginning of his early tale "The Threefold Destiny" in 1838: "I
have sometimes produced a singular and not unpleasing effect, so
far as my own mind was concerned, by imagining a train of incidents in which the spirit and mechanism of the fairy legend should
be combined with the characters and manners of familiar life. In

31 Scott, "On the Supernatural in Fictitious Composition," *Foreign Quarterly Review*, I (July, 1827), 62–64.
32 Scott, *The Monastery, Waverley Novels*, Opus Magnum Edition (Edinburgh, 1829–32), XVIII. xiii. xviii.
33 Bulwer-Lytton, *A Strange Story, The Novels and Romances of Sir
   Edward Bulwer Lytton* (London, 1863), XI, vi–vii.
34 *Literary World*, I (April, 1847), 247.

the little tale which follows, a subdued tinge of the wild and won-
derful is thrown over a sketch of New England personages and
scenery, yet, it is hoped, without entirely obliterating the sober
hues of nature." [35] And again in his late romance *The Marble Faun*,
in explanation of Donatello, his marvelous faun and natural man:
"[The author] had hoped to mystify this anomalous creature between the Real and the Fantastic, in such a manner that the reader's sympathies might be excited to a certain pleasurable degree,
without impelling him to ask how Cuvier would have classified
poor Donatello, or to insist upon being told, in so many words,
whether he had furry ears or no" (pp. 463-464). Both instances
demonstrate the typical concern of the romancer to excite the
reader's interest and to gain artistic distance through the marvelous, without entering into sheer fantasy.

When distinguishing the romance from the novel in his Preface
to *The House of the Seven Gables*, Hawthorne suggests caution in
using the marvelous. It ought to appear only "as a slight, delicate,
and evanescent flavor," he states. Yet in his tales he experimented
widely. At one extreme, in "Feathertop," he gives a straightforward albeit whimsical depiction of Mother Rigby's supernatural creation of a lifelike scarecrow. At the other extreme, in
"Lady Eleanore's Mantle," he explains away the magic cloak as a
smallpox carrier. Between these extremes is "The Prophetic Pictures," in which Hawthorne's wizard artist foretells the future of
Walter and Elinor Ludlow by looking into their "inmost souls,"
his power being a blend of human canniness and extrasensory perception. This middle way, following the romancer's balance, was
most typical of Hawthorne in his longer fiction.

The marvelous events in *The Scarlet Letter* are ambiguous.
Rarely does Hawthorne describe them objectively. Yet the romance is filled with the "evanescent flavor" of the marvelous as
seen by the superstitious New Englanders of the seventeenth century. Roger Chillingworth and Pearl have supernatural dimensions.
Mistress Hibbins is a portrait of a historical person considered a
witch. And the letter *A* takes on supernatural properties to the ex-

35 *Works,* I, 527.

tent that Hester comes to regard it almost as a talisman or binding charm.

Essentially, we could consider Roger Chillingworth a sorcerer. He gives himself the suggestive title of alchemist. He could also be described as a doctor of skill, because of his scientific background in Europe and his study of herbs in America. However, the author stresses not his ability and knowledge, but the superstitious wonder directed at his ability and knowledge by the Puritans: "He was heard to speak of Sir Kenelm Digby, and other famous men,—whose scientific attainments were esteemed hardly less than supernatural..." (p. 121). Rumors are circulated by the townspeople about the "black art" Chillingworth learned from the Indians. Hence, some of the townspeople fear him to be an emissary of Satan. Early in the romance, Hester fears the potion he makes for Pearl, and, although her fear is groundless, it does focus attention on Chillingworth's skill with drugs and prepares the reader for the medicine he devises later with evil intent for Dimmesdale. Since Chillingworth uses his black plants from a dead man's heart to increase Dimmesdale's fear of being exposed and since he uses his medicine in general to keep Dimmesdale alive only to prolong torture of him, Chillingworth's herbs and medicines are, in a real sense, evil potions, and Chillingworth is, in moral terms, what the townspeople fear him to be—an evil sorcerer sent from the devil.

More specifically, Chillingworth is identified with the Black Man of the Forest. Hawthorne explains the figure as part of "a common superstition of the period." The Black Man records the names of those who give their souls to the devil. Chillingworth is first equated with the Black Man when Hester, in prison, asks, "Art thou like the Black Man that haunts the forest round about us? Has thou enticed me into a bond that will prove the ruin of my soul?" (p. 77). This notion is reinforced at Governor Bellingham's house when Mistress Hibbins announces she has promised Hester's soul to the Black Man. In the same vein, Pearl warns her mother against Chillingworth: "Come away, or yonder old Black Man will catch you!" (p. 134). Alone with her daughter, Hester confesses that she has known the Black Man and that the scarlet letter is his mark. Here she refers to sin in general, but her choice of metaphor keeps alive the connection Hawthorne has created in the reader's mind between Chillingworth and the Black Man. Externally, Chillingworth grows darker throughout the romance. Internally, he comes to regard himself as Dimmesdale's dark fiend. And Dimmesdale, in turn, comes to think of him as the "dark and terrible old man" sent as an agent to bring Dimmesdale to his "triumphant ignominy" of dying repentance. Hawthorne, in the role of speculating editor, describes Chillingworth attempting to stop Dimmesdale's confession in similar terms: "At this instant old Roger Chillingworth thrust himself through the crowd,—or, perhaps, so dark, disturbed, and evil was his look, he rose up out of some nether region,—to snatch back his victim from what he sought to do!" (p. 252). Chillingworth, the human actor, is thus given an elaborate supernatural, or marvelous, extension. This increases his distance from the world of the reader and makes him more clearly an element in a self-consciously artificial romance world.

Pearl also is set at the distance of the marvelous. When the convex mirror at Governor Bellingham's house distorts Pearl's figure, Hester, burdened with guilt, feels "as if it could not be the image of her own child, but of an imp who was seeking to mould itself into Pearl's shape" (p. 106). The fantasies of Pearl lead Mr. Wilson to conclude, "The little baggage hath witchcraft in her.... She needs no old woman's broomstick to fly withal!" (p. 116). On the other hand, Dimmesdale, who sermonizes on the relationship of the transitory and heavenly realms, sees Pearl standing on the opposite bank of a stream as a representation of purity and grace from the heavenly realm, almost as a medieval iconographic representation. Many of the supernatural interpretations or attributes given to Pearl, then, are products of the minds of those looking at her.

The same, of course, is true of the marvelous attributes of the scarlet letter. The townspeople, watching Hester return to prison, whisper that they see "a lurid gleam" from the letter. It seems to them to cast a "spell," because of what it represents and because of how striking Hester fashioned it to be. Hester thinks herself "absolutely hidden behind it" when she sees the exaggerated version of the letter, mentioned earlier, in Bellingham's convex mirror. The meteor which marks the sky with an *A* is taken by Dimmesdale as a sign of his guilt, while to others of Boston it signifies only "Angel" for Governor Winthrop. The townspeople at the end of the romance either see or do not see the *A* on Dimmesdale's chest, depending on the attitude each one brings to the event. The supernatural elements arise from the minds of the onlookers. This is the traditional solution to the problem of balancing the marvelous and the natural. Yet we should note that Hawthorne surpasses the practice, if not the intentions, of other romancers, in that his use of the marvelous is not just to arouse wonder and create artistic distance, but to externalize attitudes of his characters and thereby contribute to his idealization of them.

Many of the supernatural elements in *The House of the Seven Gables* are created in order to be destroyed. They constitute the mystery from the past that the characters in the present must solve before they can end the feud between the Maule family and the Pyncheon family. Certainly an important part of the process of bridging the gulf between the two families is Holgrave's explanation of Maule's curse. The four mysterious deaths in the Pyncheon line, Holgrave believes, resulted from a hereditary illness usually attacking "in the tension of some mental crisis." Maule's curse— "God will give him blood to drink"—was "founded on a knowledge of this predisposition." Further, Holgrave explains that Matthew Maule's witchcraft and the grandson's spell on Alice Pyncheon were no more than the results of mesmerism (an explanation hinted by Hawthorne early in the romance). What Holgrave does not explain, Hawthorne does. The enchanted well was made brackish by the cellar Colonel Pyncheon dug. The power of Colonel Pyncheon's portrait over Clifford comes from Clifford's half-remembered knowledge of the treaty concealed behind it. Only Hawthorne's fantasy of the ghosts visiting on the night of Judge Pyncheon's death cannot be dismissed with a natural explanation, and here Hawthorne begs the reader to accept his "brief extravagance" as an authorial intrusion into the fabric of the story. The intrusion is significant. We shall have to return to the scene later, for it demonstrates Hawthorne's self-conscious use of artifice to break or suspend verisimilitude. But for the moment, we may consider it an exception to his general handling of the marvelous. Most of the marvelous events are explained away. At the same time, their effects on the characters are very important. The superstitions and legends associated with the house are Hawthorne's main vehicles for carrying the actual wrongs between the two families from the past into the present. Yet Hawthorne, in the very voice with which he presents the superstitions, tends to mock them as quaint beliefs from the past that are not acceptable in the present. He uses the marvelous as a means to irony.

The same is true in *The Blithedale Romance*. Here Hawthorne works through the extravagant imagination of his narrator, Miles Coverdale. Coverdale begins by expressing his curiosity about the Veiled Lady, "phenomenon in the mesmeric line." When he meets Priscilla, he regards her as "some desolate kind of a creature, doomed to wander about in snow-storms," who has been "tempted" into a "human dwelling." Similarly, he sees Zenobia as an enchantress: "She is a sister of the Veiled Lady! That flower in her hair is a talisman. If you were to snatch it away, she would vanish, or be transformed into something else!" (p. 45). Hollingsworth's relation to Priscilla he sees as that of "dragon" to "maiden." Westervelt appears first to Coverdale as "the salvage man of antiquity, hirsute and cinctured with a leafy girdle," and takes on various satanic forms for Coverdale, until he learns Westervelt's real identity as magician—a profession about which Coverdale has heard "stranger stories than ever were written in a romance." Moodie is "the wretchest old ghost in the world." And in his fever, Coverdale even suspects himself of being a "mesmerical clairvoyant." The irony is multi-level. In the first place, Coverdale's fanciful way of seeing the characters hinders his ability to find out the "facts" of the situations they are involved in. And yet, on another level, many of his fancies turn out to be extremely accurate metaphors for the actualities.

Of all the characters, Zenobia takes Coverdale's musings the

most seriously. At first she mocks the "supernatural machinery"
he puts around Priscilla's entrance at the farm house, and she
laughs at his idea of her as an enchantress: "I scorn to owe anything to magic" (p. 45). But as she becomes aware of Priscilla's
hold on her, she adopts the language of Coverdale's fantasies. Her
legend of Priscilla's ability as the Veiled Lady is told in terms
"something so nearly like a ghost story . . . that you shall hardly
tell the difference." She thinks herself tried for "Witchcraft" by
Hollingsworth. Priscilla becomes her "evil fate." She vows to
"haunt" Hollingsworth. And she passes on her flower to Priscilla
with the curse, "she must soon fade." Thus Zenobia picks up and
extends Coverdale's fantasies. These two points of view, along
with mesmerism and stage magic, give the romance a consistent
layer of the marvelous. It consists mainly in the verbal texture,
rather than the action of the romance. To some extent Coverdale
and Zenobia are merely indulging their imaginations with the vocabulary of the supernatural, but also, to a greater extent, they use
the vocabulary wittily to express attitudes about the other characters that are too puzzling, often too frightening, to be spelled out
more clearly. The final irony of the romance is that the fantasies
of Coverdale and Zenobia tend to come true, because their original
insights, cloaked in the language of the marvelous, were valid.

The Marble Faun depends the most heavily of Hawthorne's
four major romances on the balance of the marvelous and the natural. The artistic center of the work is Donatello's ritualistic fall
from innocence to experience. Against this archetypal ritual Hawthorne sets his travel-book observations of Italy, in order to adjust the work's distance from the reader's world. Similarly, to
control his distance, he parallels the action in the novel's present
with marvelous legends and beliefs from the past. The appearance
of Miriam's model, for instance, is linked with the legend of the
persecutor haunting the catacomb. The model himself reinforces
this idea (after being confronted by Kenyon) by describing himself as a spectral persecutor: "Inquire not what I am, nor where-
fore I abide in the darkness. . . . Henceforth, I am nothing but a
shadow behind her footsteps. She came to me when I sought her

not. She has called me forth, and must abide the consequences of my re-appearance in the world" (p. 31). The blood that trickles from his nostrils after he has died, although adequately explained by Kenyon as "not yet congealed blood," seems to guilt-stricken Miriam a sign of his supernatural power to name his murderer.

Monte Beni is also surrounded with marvelous legends. Because of guilt, Donatello seizes on the English necromancer's belief that the tower was once a prison. He thinks of his Sunshine wine as an "ethereal potation" or a means of escape from remorse. The legend of the nymph of the fountain frightens him because it parallels his relationship with Miriam, and the alabaster copy of the skull of the knight who lost the fountain-lady, in particular, increases his torment as a possible foreshadowing of the futility of his love.

The characters of *The Marble Faun* see a supernatural dimension frequently in works of art. Donatello finds "witchcraft" in Miriam's self-portrait. Miriam calls Hilda's Beatrice Cenci a "magical picture" because of the mystery of the soul caught by Hilda. A haunting resemblance between Guido's sketch of the demon and the face of Miriam's model is recognized by Kenyon, Hilda, and Donatello. Finally, Kenyon's "accidental handling of the clay" of Donatello's bust amazes both Kenyon and Donatello by the "distorted and violent look" given to the faun.

Near the end of the romance, Hawthorne advises the reader not to separate the mysterious from the real, the marvelous from the natural. "The gentle reader, we trust, would not thank us for one of those minute elucidations, which are so tedious, and, after all, so unsatisfactory, in clearing up the romantic mysteries of a story. He is too wise to insist upon looking closely at the wrong side of the tapestry, after the right one has been sufficiently displayed to him, woven with the best of the artist's skill, and cunningly arranged with a view to the harmonious exhibition of its colours" (p. 455). Hawthorne uses no irony in *The Marble Faun*. Yet the presence of the marvelous does contribute to his self-conscious handling of artifice. The legends of the past and the imaginative projections of the characters put the narrative into the realm of the supernatural. More important, however, the marvelous events serve to parallel the events in which the characters participate. They provide the sense of a repetitive dimension that is necessary if the reader is to see Hawthorne's "tapestry" as ritualistic. At the high level of ritual, the supernatural and the realistic are, indeed, all one.

History gave the nineteenth-century romancer his simplest solution to the problem of artistic distance. A fictional work could be set off from the world of the reader through time. Such a work would have the advantage, over straightforward history, of fictional shaping. In America as early as 1800, Charles Brockden Brown laid out fundamental definitions for the balance in his article "The Difference between History and Romance": "The observer or experimentalist, therefore, who carefully watches and carefully enumerates the appearances which occur may claim the appellation of historian. He who adorns these appearances with cause and effect, and traces resemblances between the past, distant, and future, with the present, performs a different part. He is a dealer, not in certainties, but probabilities, and is therefore a romancer." [36] Converting Aristotle's famous distinction between poetry and history to new ends, Brown states that the historian merely records facts, whereas the romancer deals, in broad, human terms, with the connections between the facts. Furthermore, Brown insists, later in his essay, that the romancer must break down each individual historical fact into its "series of motives and incidents" as well as make clear the pattern of meaning created by the relationships among the historical facts. That such aims were too difficult for most, if not all, romancers was irrelevant to Brown. The goal was there to be sought.

His kind of distinction became widespread. Exactly the same conclusion about the difference between the historian and the romancer was reached by Cooper in his 1823 Preface to *The Pilot*, by William Craig Brownlee in the romance *The Whigs of Scotland* in 1833, and by William Gilmore Simms in his 1845 collec-

36 Brown, "The Difference between History and Romance," *Monthly Magazine and American Review*, II (April, 1800), 251.

tion of essays, *Views and Reviews in American Literature*. In *Notions of the Americans*, however, Cooper—as the *North American Review* writers Channing, Tudor, and Knapp did before him and Hawthorne was to do after him—raised the issue whether the brevity of American history precluded the artistic distance needed by the romancer.[37] Debate on this later issue kept the romancer's balance of history and fiction in the forefront of critical discussions of American fiction.

Again, however, it was the British writers Scott and Bulwer-Lytton who commented the most fully on techniques for achieving the balance. According to Scott in his Dedicatory Epistle to *Ivanhoe*, romances take place in "that extensive neutral ground, that is, of manners and sentiments which are common to us and to our ancestors, having been handed down unaltered from them to us."[38] Using the analogy of the painter, Scott explains further the romancer's proper business:

> The painter must introduce no ornament inconsistent with the climate or country of his landscape; he must not plant cypress trees upon Inch-Merrin, or Scots firs among the ruins of Persepolis; and the author lies under a corresponding restraint. However far he may venture in a more full detail of passions and feelings, than is to be found in the ancient compositions which he imitates, he must introduce nothing inconsistent with the manners of the age; his knights, squires, grooms, and yeomen may be more fully drawn than in the hard, dry delineations of an ancient illuminated manuscript, but the character and costume of the age must remain inviolate.... His language must not be exclusively obsolete and unintelligible; but he should admit, if possible, no word or turn of phraseology betraying an origin directly modern.[39]

The romancer should consider his "neutral ground" bounded by historical facts. But within this boundary he may imaginatively picture his conception of human experience. It is a general human

---

37 Cooper, *Notions of the Americans: Picked up by a Travelling Bachelor* (Philadelphia, 1828), II, 111–112. The arguments of Channing, Tudor, Knapp, and Hawthorne are treated by Orians in "The Romance Ferment."

38 Scott, *Ivanhoe, Waverley Novels*, XVI, xxxiv.

39 *Ibid.*, p. xxxix.

experience, similar to all epochs, that Scott aims for. The romancer's language should be from a general or basic English vocabulary
which Scott stated was unchanged, except in spelling, from Chau-
cer's time. To insure that the bounds of historical facts were not
too confining, Scott used famous historical personages only in the
background of his romances. Such he did, for instance, with Richard the Lionhearted in *Ivanhoe*. Scott justified many periods of
history as suitable to the romancer's needs. He defended, for instance, the reign of James I because it was a time when remnants
of chivalry co-existed with modern manners to form an era removed from the modern one, but not too far removed.[40] He liked
also the recent history of Scotland, since to his English readers the
history was cloaked in the aura of legend, yet closely tied up with
their own history.[41] Also, Scotland contained the extremes of sophistication and of belief in the supernatural. And finally, the
Scottish dialect worked nicely along with the romancer's basic
English vocabulary. The dialect, used sparingly, could help establish the work's distance.

Bulwer-Lytton, in the Preface to *Harold*, distinguished between
two methods of using history in romance: "the one consists in
lending to ideal personages, and to an imaginary fable, the addi-
tional interest to be derived from historical groupings; the other
in extracting the main interest of romantic narrative from history
itself." [42] The first method, he felt, was Scott's; the second, Bulwer-Lytton's own. Opposed to Scott, Bulwer-Lytton insisted the
romancer could treat important historical figures as major characters. The freedom needed for fiction, he argued, could come from
the writer's concentration on the "inward" lives of his characters, rather than their "public and historical" lives. On the subject
of language, he agreed generally with Scott's "compromise between the modern and the elder diction," [43] but he did insist on his
right to use anachronisms when modern language provided no

40 Scott, *The Fortunes of Nigel, Waverley Novels*, XXVI, vi–vii.
41 Scott, *Waverley, Waverley Novels*, I, x; *The Antiquary*, V, i–ii; *Rob Roy*, VII, viii.
42 Bulwer-Lytton, *Harold, Novels and Romances*, VII, viii.
43 Bulwer-Lytton, *The Last of the Barons, Novels and Romances*, VI, v.

equivalent for the words he needed.[44] Despite these differences, both men were absolutely agreed that the romancer needed to define a "neutral ground" within the confines of historical facts where he could offer his abstracted picture of human experience. In this "neutral ground," at a distance from contemporary readers, the romancer could expect his picture to be more clearly seen.

Directly in the tradition of the historical romancers is Hawthorne with his remarks at the beginning of his biographical sketch "Sir William Phips." He attacks good-humoredly the practice of historians and biographers of doing no more than listing historical facts and states the need for imaginative handling of history.

> The knowledge communicated by the historian and biographer is analogous to that which we acquire of a country by the map,—minute, perhaps, and accurate, and available for all necessary purposes, but cold and naked, and wholly destitute of the mimic charm produced by landscape-painting. These defects are partly remediable, and even without an absolute violation of literal truth, although by methods rightfully interdicted to professors of biographical exactness. A license must be assumed in brightening the materials which time has rusted, and in tracing out half-obliterated inscriptions on the columns of antiquity: Fancy must throw her reviving light on the faded incidents that indicate character, whence a ray will be reflected, more or less vividly, on the person to be described.[45]

The "license" Hawthorne claims here is exactly the freedom Brown, Scott, and Bulwer-Lytton claimed for the romancer in order to distinguish him from the historian. Less stridently, he is calling for their balance of history and fictional shaping.

This attitude continued throughout Hawthorne's entire career, but it is especially prominent in his early writing. In "Dr. Bullivant" he whimsically fabricates the adventures of Benjamin Bullivant, a supporter of Andros arrested in the Puritan revolt of 1689, in order, he claims, to "give a species of distinctness and point to some remarks on the tone and composition of New England society," and in his Preface to *Grandfather's Chair* Hawthorne tells us of his desire to make the figures of history "assume the hues of

44 Bulwer-Lytton, *Harold, Novels and Romances*, VII, v.
45 *Works*, XII, 227.

life" so that children may enjoy stories of their historical heritage. With "Roger Malvin's Burial" and "The Maypole of Merry Mount" he prefaces his fiction with brief discussions of the suitability of the historical situations to the romancer's needs, and with such tales as "The Gentle Boy," "The Gray Champion," and "Endicott and the Red Cross" he begins with historical sketches of the eras he treats in order to call attention to the work's distance. Similarly, his celebrated and disturbing tale "My Kinsman, Major Molineux," whatever its levels of psychological appeal, takes its start in the author's opening remarks on the historical situation in Massachusetts after the revocation of the early charter. Hawthorne uses the situation of the American turning against or "betraying" his English "kinsman" and his English past.

Such methods of beginning are as much a part of the tradition of the romance as the opening declaration of a moral. In "The Legends of the Province House," a work somewhat later than those just mentioned, we begin to find Hawthorne mocking this kind of conventional opening just as he mocked the declaration of a moral. Hawthorne's persona looks around the Province House, "striving with the best energy of . . . imagination, to throw a tinge of romance and historic grandeur over the realities of the scene." Far from achieving his purpose, he is instead overcome by the cigar smoke of his garrulous acquaintance, Bela Tiffany. Before recounting Tiffany's story of a painting which used to hang in the Province House, the persona confesses, "The following is as correct a version of the fact as the reader would be likely to obtain from any other source, although, assuredly, it has a tinge of romance approaching to the marvellous." [46] The persona switches from an exuberant search for a "tinge of romance" to a somewhat shamefaced admission that such a "tinge" exists in good proportion in his tales. Eventually, after four tales have been told, the persona is so confused and caught up by the "dreams of the past" that he flees the Province House, "resolved not to show my face in the Province House for a good while hence—if ever," in a flight to keep his sanity. The whole elaborate framework of the Prov-

46 *Works*, I, 293.

ince House is presented facetiously. It calls attention to the artifice of the tales. The reader is made quite aware that he is being led into the historical past only on the level of fable.

This inversion of a romance convention appears in a more subtle and more successful form in "The Custom-House" section of Hawthorne's *The Scarlet Letter*. There Hawthorne works to prepare the reader for the balance of history and fiction in the body of the work. He treats ironically the device of the discovered manuscript made famous by Walpole in *The Castle of Otranto* and imitated by many others. First Hawthorne tells the reader that his search through the documents of the Salem Custom House has yielded some worthwhile "materials of local history," but he hastily adds that these materials concern a period later than the one he is going to treat in his romance. Then, when he uncovers the manuscript of Surveyor Pue, dead some eighty years before the discovery, Hawthorne is quick to point out that the manuscript deals with events before Pue's birth. The document about the life of Hester Prynne is based on nothing firmer than the "oral testimony" of aged persons. Last, Hawthorne declares that he has taken imaginative liberties with the outline of Pue's data. With superb irony, Hawthorne asks his readers to consider *The Scarlet Letter* as a fictionalization of the brief documents gathered by an obscure surveyor from the memories of old people about an epoch which is only sparsely recorded in the Custom House! The result of this amusingly elaborate process is that Hawthorne manages to make quite clear the imaginative "license" of the self-conscious artist at the same time that he succeeds in calling attention to the historicity of the work. Hawthorne's tone is exactly right. He is not as falsely pious in invoking history as in his early tales, nor is he as self-deprecating as in "The Legends of the Province House." Unquestionably, Hawthorne directed *The Scarlet Letter* at his heritage, at his ancestors, as an indictment of their severity. In this rich sense it is historical. It seeks to interpret a historical era. But Hawthorne insists the readers be aware that they are receiving his conceptualization of history, not history itself.

In the body of *The Scarlet Letter* Hawthorne continues to keep

the reader aware of the historical distance. He uses several historical personages in minor roles: Governor John Winthrop, Governor Richard Bellingham, the convicted witch Ann Hibbins, and
the Apostle Eliot. As Charles Ryskamp demonstrated in "The
New England Sources of *The Scarlet Letter*," Hawthorne repro-
duces the layout of Boston in 1650 given in Caleb Snow's *History
of Boston*.[47] He depicts seventeenth-century styles in clothing, in-
serts anachronistic phrases ("I trow") into the dialogue, and offers brief essays on aspects of the Puritan temperament.

The Scarlet Letter was Hawthorne's one perfect creation of the
standard historical romance among his long fiction. Having accomplished the feat, he moved on to experiment with alternative
uses of historical distance. In *The House of the Seven Gables* he
used the intermingling of the past with the present as his means
for distance. He explains in his Preface:

> The point of view in which this Tale comes under the Romantic
> definition, lies in the attempt to connect a by-gone time with the
> very Present that is flitting away from us. It is a Legend, prolonging
> itself, from an epoch now gray in the distance, down into our own
> broad daylight, and bringing along with it some of its legendary
> mist, which the Reader, according to his pleasure, may either dis-
> regard, or allow it to float almost imperceptibly about the charac-
> ters and events, for the sake of a picturesque effect [p. 2].

The legend of the Pyncheon-Maule feud parallels and influences
the action in the contemporary era. It also provides a historical extension to the action and therefore helps create artistic distance.
Yet Hawthorne worried that the distance was not great enough.
He wrote to his friend Horatio Bridge on January 12, 1851: "It
[*The House of the Seven Gables*] has undoubtedly one disadvan-
tage, in being brought so close to the present time; whereby its
romantic improbabilities become more glaring."[48] Experimentation with historical distance presented him with difficulties. The
delicateness with which it had to be handled demanded great care.

47 Ryskamp, "The New England Sources of *The Scarlet Letter*," *American Literature*, XXXI (November, 1959), 257–272.
48 Quoted in George Parsons Lathrop, *A Study of Hawthorne* (Boston,
1876), p. 228.

In *The Blithedale Romance* he chose to avoid the problem. His alternative to historical distance here is the separation between the workings of the utopian community and the world of Hawthorne's general reading public. His fictionalization of Brook Farm, he insists, is "to establish a theatre, a little removed from the highway of ordinary travel." Hawthorne emphasizes the separation in the opening sections of the romance. When Miles Coverdale and his companions leave the town, they travel "a desolate extent of road." Footprints are covered by the falling snow. Travelers on the road offer no greeting to Coverdale's party. Snowdrifts pile up above the windows at Blithedale. For Coverdale, feverish in the night, the snowy landscape outside looks "like a lifeless copy of the world in marble." He is isolated from the familiar life in the town. This uniqueness of the world at the utopian community provides Hawthorne with an alternative to historical distance.

But with *The Marble Faun* Hawthorne returned to the kind of experimentation with history initiated in *The House of the Seven Gables*. Hawthorne states that his aim is "not to meddle with history—with which our narrative is no otherwise concerned, than that the very dust of Rome is historic, and inevitably settles on our page, and mingles with our ink" (p. 101). But in fact his conscious manipulation of history is extensive. Through the ruins, sculpture, and art of Italy, Hawthorne achieves again historical parallels for the events which take place in the work's present time, just as he did in *The House of the Seven Gables*. The difference here, as Hawthorne tells us in his Preface, is that the long history of Italy permits him to trace his parallels back to the legends of antiquity, whereas the brief history of America confined him to "a common-place prosperity, in broad and simple daylight." In other words, the long history of Italy made available a greater distance more suited to Hawthorne's need for a "neutral ground" for the artifice of romance.

Typically, Hawthorne establishes his distance at the outset. The four major characters are first presented to the reader in one of the salons of the sculpture gallery in the Capitol at Rome. The sculpture in the room and the ruins seen from one of the windows re-create "the massiveness of the Roman Past." The characters have spread out before them the flow of history—the contemporary era, the Gothic Age, the Roman Empire, the Etruscan Age, and the mythic Golden Age. As situations emerge that parallel each other each in a different age, we get the sense that we are witnessing, along with the characters, the emergence of archetypal situations which occur over and over throughout an incredibly long span of history. In this light, the interplay of the historical background and the action in the present becomes a part of an attempt by Hawthorne to escape time altogether and enter the world of artifice. He is trying to move toward a universal setting in which to stage his moral and psychological drama of the fall of man. He is pushing the idea of historical distance to its ultimate possible use—the creation of a universal realm controlled by the artist's conceptual attitudes about experience.

Ready at hand to Hawthorne were a variety of American romances that provided him with examples of how distance could be achieved through a combination of the three kinds of balances we have been examining. The difficulty with the popular romances of Hawthorne's era was that most of the writers failed to profit fully from the kind of distance they could create. They were able to arrange experience into conceptualized patterns, but were unable to do more than produce black-and-white moral conflicts between groups of characters as a result of these patterns. What the popular romancers lacked was Hawthorne's awareness that, while the diffuseness of human experience was simplified in the romance, the quality of the writer's argument about the selected elements of experience could still be very complex. While most popular romancers were prepared to stop with the creation of a world of artifice, Hawthorne wished to use his world of artifice, in effect, to debate human experience. Hawthorne's materials for such a goal, however, were inherent in the popular romances.

When Hawthorne wrote *The Scarlet Letter* he was pursuing a conflict that had received attention in other romances. Quite naturally New England history appealed to American writers. Parts of the history were sufficiently removed for readers to see the historical situations objectively and sufficiently shrouded in legend and superstition for them to feel the history exciting, but close enough to the contemporary era for readers to find the situations relevant to their experience. In other words, it could fulfill the kinds of demands Walter Scott sought in a historical epoch. Invariably, the New England romance concerned harsh Puritanism and some form of witchcraft or superstitiousness. The first, I think, because of the almost universal interest readers take in the conflict of repression and individual freedom, and the second, quite obviously, for a distancing effect. If we consider only the works of writers who, like Hawthorne, explicitly called themselves romancers, we find two New England romances in the 1820's: James McHenry's *The Spectre of the Forest ... A New England Romance* (1823) and the anonymous *The Witch of New England* (1824). But then in the 1840's, the decade before *The Scarlet Letter*, we find seven more: Henry William Herbert's trilogy, *Ruth Whalley; or, The Fair Puritan. A Romance of the Bay Province* (1844), *The Innocent Witch ... A Romance of the Bay Province* (1845), and *The Revolt of Boston ... A Romance of the Bay Province* (1845); Justin Jones's *The Young Refugee ... A Romance of New England* (1846); Harry Halyard's *The Haunted Bride; or, The Witch of Gallows Hill. A Romance of Olden Time* (1848) and *The Rover of the Reef. A Romance of Massachusetts Bay* (1848); and John Lothrop Motley's *Merry-Mount: A Romance of the Massachusetts Colony* (1849).[49]

In the early work *The Witch of New England*, we can see clearly some of the typical situations and devices of the New England romance. To get into witchcraft and New England life in the 1690's, the author used the Gothic device of the discovered manuscript as Hawthorne was later to do wryly in *The Scarlet Letter*. The central situation of the work is a clash between a woman named Annie Brown, who is thought to be a witch, and the Puritan community that bans her. The community is epitomized by the author's portrait of a Puritan, Reverend Bradley:

49 My list is gleaned from Wright's *American Fiction, 1774–1850*.

> The elder Bradley, was a tall gaunt figure, stooping and awkward;
> —a down cast eye with large black, bushy brows, gave a sinister and
> by no means agreeable expression to his countenance;—and his
> straight, black hair crossed with true Presbyterian exactness, did
> not help to soften the dark and midnight character of his face,—still
> its expression was lighted and even altered by a smile that at times
> wandered over it, and exhibited teeth regular and of excellent white-
> ness. . . . But he was superstitious, narrow minded—and in the prose-
> cution of a favorite doctrine—or in the execution of mistaken duty,—
> unrelenting, obstinate and cruel.[50]

Bradley is an idealized type which we could term the "black Puritan," because of his somberness and because of his severity. Not
important in this romance as a character who acts, he represents
the general attitude of unyielding harshness pervasive in the community, which is the force behind the town's battle with its witch.

The romance is made up of a series of episodes interspersed with
historical set pieces to establish distance, as in a more constrained
way is *The Scarlet Letter*. This romance begins with the unlikely
meeting of Edward Bradley, who is the minister's son, his friend
Charles Chesterly, and Uncas, an Indian made famous by New
England historians and used by Cooper later in *The Wept of
Wish-ton-Wish*.[51] The first episode is replete with a fall from a
cliff and the kidnapping of Edward's sister Agnes by a hostile Indian. After Agnes is rescued by Chesterly and Uncas, the focus
shifts to Annie, the so-called witch, and her friend Mike Shuck,
who clash with the townspeople and abduct two children. At this
point the two lines of plot converge: Annie and Mike help the
hostile Indian escape from jail, and they unite with the Indian's
tribe against the Puritans. But the author stops this development to
introduce Edward Whalley, the English regicide living as a hermit in a cave in New England, to discourse on the air of mystery
of the American Indian, and to sketch a typical Quaker. Then the

50 *The Witch of New England; A Romance* (Philadelphia, 1824), pp. 30–31.
51 This Uncas is of a much earlier generation than the Mohican chief who
    was to be popularized by Cooper in the Leatherstocking Tales. But this
    Uncas was well known in American legends through the work of the
    New England historians.

plot speeds to its conclusion: Annie and the Indians attack the Puritans; Edward falls captive, but escapes into the arms of Whalley's daughter; Annie is captured; and in a concluding scene which prefigures Hawthorne's first scaffold scene in *The Scarlet Letter*, the Puritans converse by the prison door about the marriage of Charles to Agnes and Edward to Whalley's daughter while they watch Annie taken to the gallows. Crude as the romance is, it does demonstrate the American romancer's attempt to gain artistic distance by using historical details, and it does offer what we may call a central situation in the New England romance —the individual alienated from the Puritan community.

This central situation took more definite shape in the romances of the 1840's, and certain type characters suggested in the earlier romance became more prominent. The most obvious villain was the "black Puritan," and the most clear-cut heroine was his opposite, the "fair Puritan." Both types have major roles in Henry William Herbert's trilogy on Ruth Whalley, the fictional granddaughter of the regicide. Herbert's "fair Puritan" is surely derived from the heroines of sentimental literature, but she differs from them in that she is presented in the very specific context of strict Puritanism. She defines her "fairness" by opposing the severity of the Puritan world with her virtues of compassion and sympathy. The harsh "blackness" of her Puritan father, ironically named Merciful, makes Ruth's "fairness" more clear. Dressed in a black jerkin, with a dark, lined face, thin lips, and a sharp, aquiline nose, Merciful Whalley represents the same figure as does Reverend Bradley. His heart is too hard. In his fanatical zeal to convert to Puritanism the Indian servant Tituba, Merciful drives the Indian girl to attack him, and then, with obvious relish, he flogs her almost to death as punishment. In contrast, Ruth gives the Indian girl so much kindness and understanding that when Tituba has the chance to gain revenge on Whalley by telling the king's troops where to find the regicide, Tituba holds back her information.

Herbert insisted on the importance of the historical boundaries of the world of his romance. In the Preface to his trilogy he stated:

> This, the only *American* Romance of the author, is truly a his-
> torical romance; many of the persons being genuine historical char-
> acters, and the facts generally and the spirit of the age carefully
> preserved. The period is one of the most interesting of the early
> times of North American history, being that of the subsidence of the
> terrible excitement of the Salem witchcraft, the tyrannous govern-
> ment of Sir Edmund Andros, and the first organized and successful
> resistence to the authority of the crown.[52]

But history in this romance is mostly a means to props which establish a highly artificial, highly contrived fictional world. The action of the trilogy is set in 1688. Its ending depends on the historical event of the overthrow of Andros as Governor of the Bay
Province. After the episodes about Tituba, Herbert introduces
Andros as a repressive tyrant (almost a political equivalent to the
religious tyrant Merciful Whalley) who comes to the Whalley
home to seize Ruth's grandfather and, failing that, takes Ruth for
a hostage and mistress. When Ruth refuses his seductions, Andros
has Puritan magistrates condemn her for witchcraft. Before she
can be executed, however, the colonists revolt against Andros and
put him to flight. Merciful Whalley is killed during the confusion
of Andros' escape, leaving Ruth free to develop and expand her
capacities for love for the first time.

The work is highly artificial in that we see the characters only
from the outside as general types. In Ruth's case, we deduce her
character primarily from the responses she gets from the people
around her. The wild servant Tituba gives her a fierce loyalty; her
harsh father softens a little before her when Ruth intercedes for
the Indian; Henry Cecil, a soldier in the king's army, resigns his
commission to defend her when she is taken captive; Andros lusts
for her; and the jailer of Boston is so moved by her innocence that
he protects her from the assaults of Andros. In Merciful Whalley's case, we deduce his character from his appearance, described
above, and his actions, such as his superstitious cringing from a

---

52 Herbert, Author's Preface, *The Fair Puritan. An Historical Romance
   of the Days of Witchcraft* (Philadelphia, 1875), n. p. The trilogy re-
   printed in this late edition is the only text known to be still extant.

bloody footprint planted on his cloak by Tituba. Both Ruth and Merciful are type characters participating as extremes in the central situations of a sympathetic, loving nature alienated from, or in conflict with, Puritan severity. They embody the ideal pattern of "fair Puritan" versus "black Puritan." But Herbert can do no more with this pattern than offer the melodramatic overthrow of all the forces of repression. He cannot put to use the world of artifice he so elaborately builds.

The New England romance dealing with the same central situation, which used the balances of romance theory the most carefully, was historian John Lothrop Motley's *Merry-Mount*. His work is almost a guidebook for romance distance. Motley went back into New England history further than the other romancers and singled out the pre-colonial days as well suited to the romancer's need for a "neutral ground": "The crepuscular period which immediately preceded the rise of Massachusetts Colony, possesses more of the elements of romance than any subsequent epoch. After the arrival of Winthrop with the charter, the history of the province is as clear day-light; but during the few previous years there are several characters flitting like phantoms through the chronicles of the time. . . ." [53] Following Scott and Bulwer-Lytton, Motley was concerned to find an era where he would be free to fictionalize within the boundary of historical facts. His romance has two main plots. One is largely historical: the conflict between Thomas Morton's band of revelers on Mount Wollaston and the Puritans under the leadership of Standish and Endicott. The other is largely fictional: the troubled love affair of Esther Ludlow, a young Puritan girl, and Henry Maudsley, the son of wealthy Church of England parents. The villain, Sir Christopher Gardiner, who comes between Maudsley and Esther and promotes strife between the revelers and the Puritans, is the main link between the plots. He is presented as the son of the historical figure Ferdinando Gorges, and he helps, therefore, to establish Motley's balance of history and fiction. Moreover, various historical vignettes

53 Motley, *Merry-Mount; A Romance of the Massachusetts Colony* (Boston and Cambridge, 1849), I, 3.

—descriptions of Standish, Endicott, and Winthrop; sections on hunting a buck, killing a wolf, and falconing; re-enactments of the May Day celebrations at Mount Wollaston and of Puritan trials —contribute to this balance.

As was to be the case with Hawthorne in *The Scarlet Letter*, the marvelous events in *Merry-Mount* often result from the superstitiousness of the settlers. In one section, the trail of a meteor seems to take the shape of a sword to a hermit who predicts from this "sign" the stabbing of Maudsley. The scene roughly parallels Hawthorne's use of the meteor which appears to be an *A* in the sky in *The Scarlet Letter*.

Motley's romance is peopled with type characters who act out Motley's ideal patterns. Esther Ludlow is another "fair Puritan" contrasted with intolerant Puritans who persecute the revelers too severely. (Motley uses the phrase "fair Puritan" several times for Esther.) A stronger figure than Ruth Whalley, Esther demonstrates her capacity for sympathy in a positive way by nursing the sick in the struggling settlement. The villain, Sir Christopher, resembles the "black Puritan," although he is actually an enemy to the Puritan community. He wears a "steeple-crowned hat, a short black cloak, with a white band about his throat, and other habiliments, of the color cherished by the Puritans." [54] Traveled in all corners of the world, he uses his "deep knowledge of human nature" for his own ends and thus reveals himself more overtly evil than a "black Puritan." Yet he has much in common with the hard, unyielding Puritans. At the end of the romance, the spirit of love and tolerance of the "fair Puritan" wins out equally over the evil of Sir Christopher and over the harshness of the Puritans, making the work's idealized pattern of meaning quite clear.

Popular romancers like Herbert and Motley were quite capable of creating romance distance, and they were able to isolate a central dilemma in the Puritan situation, the crisis of individual freedom versus a severely restrictive community. But they were not able to use the distance they achieved to enrich their treatment of the dilemma. This, however, was precisely what Hawthorne was

54 *Ibid.*, I, 17.

able to do. Distance provided him with the freedom to conduct a dialectical investigation of the conflict, drawing on several voices or points of view. He used the artificial world of romance as a realm where a complex questioning process could be conducted by the author, who needed to feel little compunction to disguise himself as questioner. The very artifice of the romance attested to his presence. Specifically, in *The Scarlet Letter*, Hawthorne used the central situation of the "fair Puritan" versus the "black Puritan" as the framework for his investigation of the New England past and of the generalized problem of the individual's role with a society of human beings.

Similarly in a work like *The House of the Seven Gables*, we can see Hawthorne transforming usual romance materials into a more ironic mode that again allows him to probe the materials quite self-consciously. A brief examination of a romance of revenge, *The Old Sanctuary* (1846), by Augustus Julian Requier, will make this quite clear. Requier treats the theme of a past evil bearing on a new generation as Hawthorne was to do in *The House of the Seven Gables*, but Requier has none of Hawthorne's ironic detachment from his theme.

Conventionally enough, Requier begins his work by discussing the suitability for romance of his setting along the Ashley River in South Carolina and by claiming to have derived his story from a discovered eighteenth-century manuscript. After thus trying to establish his distance, he develops his theme. Although not fully integrated into the plot, the Old Sanctuary, "dilapidated remnants, of what was probably once a family vault," is intended as a structural center for the theme. The sanctuary is the background for the meetings of the young lovers, Edward St. Julian and Blanche Rosalind. It serves as an image of decay in contrast to a rose tree blooming before it. "And, near the remains of a crumbling portico a solitary rose-tree grew up in a wild but rich luxuriance, as if to embody the familiar antithesis of beauty blooming in dreariness, of desolation. Blanche had plucked one of these flowers; and she held it almost mechanically in her left hand, which reposed carelessly upon her lap, while the other feebly grasped an angle projecting from the rude seat which she occupied." [55] This contrast is like the one between the House of the Seven Gables and the Pyncheon elm in Hawthorne's work. In both romances the image of decay is counterpoised with an image of rejuvenation. The shadow of the decaying sanctuary and of the past it represents falls on Edward and Blanche, just as the gloom of the House of the Seven Gables falls on Hawthorne's Holgrave and Phoebe. The family quarrel in the past which separates Edward and Blanche grew out of the deceit of Philip Rosalind, Blanche's father, in stealing away the woman loved by Adrian St. Julian, Edward's father, and a large portion of St. Julian's estate. Philip Rosalind had turned Adrian St. Julian's father, Edward's grandfather, against his son by means of accounts of St. Julian's profligacies, and the patriarchal father had cursed St. Julian to die "forlorn and forsaken, in the tenantless Halls of his fathers." As a result, St. Julian makes Edward swear to help him get revenge. But before this can happen, Adrian St. Julian finds Philip Rosalind covered with blood in the forest and mistakenly believes he has killed Edward. Adrian and Philip fight. A torch falls to the ground, and fire flares up. Adrian is severely burned and eventually dies, after being carried to the "tenantless Halls" of his house. Overcome with guilt and sensing his past crimes closing in on him, Philip Rosalind commits suicide. The two lovers are at last freed from the oath of vengeance between their families.

The Old Sanctuary is not offered as a source for The House of the Seven Gables, but rather as an example of a popular romance which treats a similar theme. The difference between the two works lies in Hawthorne's creation of the mock-heroic characters Hepzibah and Clifford. If those characters were missing, Hawthorne's story would be almost exactly like The Old Sanctuary, with Holgrave and Phoebe eventually shaking free from the curse of the past. But the comic and pathetic love between Hepzibah and Clifford suggests something of a mockery of such an easy solution. They burlesque the young lovers and call attention to the

55 Requier, The Old Sanctuary. A Romance of the Ashley (Boston, 1846), p. 34.

contrived nature of their resolution. The artifice, so admitted, becomes more palatable. And we as readers are prepared to look more closely at Hawthorne's argument, for clearly he is asking us to go beyond the conventional easy solution of the disappearance of the wrong from the past.

This is also apparent from Hawthorne's detached, ironic handling of conventional melodramatic scenes. In *The Old Sanctuary*, when Adrian St. Julian narrates his confrontation of his father, which leads to the father's death, the description of the scene resembles Hawthorne's depiction of the dead Colonel Pyncheon. Requier's scene is as follows:

> "I waited on my father. It was toward evening. The aged invalid sat upon a chair—" here the speaker examined that upon which he was seated, and a slight tremor might have been observed, as he continued, "the same—the very same. His brow, naturally stern and repulsive, wore a soft and subdued expression, as if the pains of disease had humbled the proud man to a sense of his comparative insignificance. . . . He stood up—the death-stricken Patriarch stood up—his voice, like the pealing thunders of Heaven, rung in my ears, as it imprecated its vengeance on my head; and a father's curse was graven eternally on my vicious heart, as he staggered and fell, bathed in his blood, upon the floor—his ghostly eyeballs fixed in life's last, agonizing struggles, on the murderer—his only child! his once beloved son." [56]

The scene is intended to be horrific. All the details work to that end—the presence of the death chair to make the story credible, the stern brow now humbled, the voice like thunder, the father's curse, the blood bath on the floor from the hemorrhage, the eyeballs fixed in death, and the son's anguish. The details are, of course, excessive, and they are utterly conventional. Yet Hawthorne uses almost exactly the same details in his depiction of Colonel Pyncheon's death and succeeds admirably. The reason is that Hawthorne manages to understate the horrific vocabulary by holding back the statement that the Colonel is dead until the end of the description. His understatement makes the scene almost comic. Hawthorne writes:

56 *Ibid.*, pp. 18–19.

...a portrait of Colonel Pyncheon, beneath which sat the original Colonel himself, in an oaken elbow-chair, with a pen in his hand. Letters, parchments, and blank sheets of paper were on the table before him. He appeared to gaze at the curious crowd, in front of which stood the Lieutenant Governor; and there was a frown on his dark and massive countenance, as if sternly resentful of the boldness that had impelled them into his private retirement.

A little boy—the Colonel's grandchild, and the only human being that ever dared to be familiar with him—now made his way among the guests and ran toward the seated figure; then pausing half-way, he began to shriek with terror. The company—tremulous as the leaves of a tree, when all are shaking together—drew nearer, and perceived that there was an unnatural distortion in the fixedness of Colonel Pyncheon's stare; that there was blood on his ruff, and that his hoary beard was saturated with it. It was too late to give assistance. The iron-hearted Puritan—the relentless persecutor—the grasping and strong-willed man—was dead! [p. 15].

Whereas Requier barrages the reader with grim details and standard conceits, Hawthorne conducts him through a range of emotions from amusement at the spellbound crowd fixed by the eyes of a grim patriarch, to horror at the abruptness of Pyncheon's death, to a mixed reaction of amusement and horror at the realization that the timorous crowd had been afraid of a powerless human shell. Hawthorne here plays on the conventionally horrific scene. But more important to note is the awareness of the reader that he is being manipulated, that an author is turning conventional materials upside down, and that the reader is in a fictional world where the author can flaunt his artifice.

Hawthorne strove for the artistic distance of the romance. To accomplish this goal, as we have seen, he used the three balances of verisimilitude and idealization, the natural and the marvelous, and history and fiction. Once he achieved his distance, however, he chose to call attention to the artifice it implied. This he did by making the reader recognize that he was entering into the process of examining human experience. In Hawthorne's four long works we can find a growing emphasis on self-conscious artifice and on the desire to involve the reader in the working out of the writer's inquiry.

This was not the case, however, with Hawthorne's first work, *Fanshawe*. This romance was published three years after Hawthorne's graduation from Bowdoin, and it demonstrates the need of the apprentice for a master. Hawthorne imitated the English Gothic romancers and Walter Scott. The action of Hawthorne's work consists mainly of the elaborate abduction of the heroine, Ellen Langton, by the traveled, mysterious villain, Butler, and the pursuit undertaken by Fanshawe, the pale scholar, Walcott, the vigorous, rash young man, and Ellen's guardian, Dr. Melmoth. Critic William Bysshe Stein has placed Hawthorne's book in the tradition of the Gothic thriller. Butler's fall from a precipice, he points out, resembles, in substance and language, the violent death of Robert Maturin's Faustian hero in *Melmoth the Wanderer*.[57] But Hawthorne's main debt is to Scott.[58] The time of Fanshawe is eighty years in the past, a "middle distance" like Scott's *Waverley, or 'Tis Sixty Years Since*. The setting around Hawthorne's Harley College, "secluded from the sight and sound of the busy world," is similar to Scott's countrysides in Scotland, contiguous to, but different from, the mannered world of civilization. Hawthorne shifts his scenes quickly from one group of characters to another in the manner of Scott, already copied in America in works like *The Witch of New England*, and, like Scott, Hawthorne plays off his low characters (the comic president of the college and the characters at a nearby inn) against the high characters (Ellen, Fanshawe, and Walcott) in order to keep the extravagant emotions of the high characters in bounds. Hawthorne's language, in particular, seems patterned on Scott's idea of a "middle diction." One critic, Robert E. Gross, has pointed out that in his descriptive

57 Stein, *Hawthorne's Faust* (Gainesville, Fla., 1953), p. 41. Hawthorne's debt to Maturin is acknowledged indirectly by Hawthorne's name for Ellen's guardian and by his quotation of some of Maturin's lines as an epigraph to Chapter 8.
58 Again Hawthorne acknowledged his debt indirectly by an epigraph, this time to Chapter 7.

passages Hawthorne strives for the poetic word: a building becomes an "edifice"; a valley, a "vale"; and a home, a "habitation"
or a "hearth." [59] Rather than merely trying to be *poetic*, it is likely
Hawthorne was struggling for a vocabulary that would remove
the action from the context of everyday experience without
breaking away too far from common speech—an effect he achieves
magnificently later.

    Distance is Hawthorne's aim in *Fanshawe*. By imitating Scott he
achieves it. However, it serves no purpose beyond escapism. The
villain dies, Walcott wins Ellen, and Fanshawe languishes toward
an early grave. The lesson of *Fanshawe* for Hawthorne was the
need to develop and use the romance distance as a means to another end, that end being self-conscious speculation on human experience. When Hawthorne came to recognize this potential in
the romance, the form became for him what other romancers had
always wanted it to be: a highly ordered, carefully patterned approach to experience.

59 Gross, "Hawthorne's First Novel: The Future of a Style," *PMLA*,
LXXVIII (March, 1963), 60.

Chapter II

The tales:
self-conscious probing for meaning
and the procession of life

Hawthorne's tales provide us with insight into his particular approach to meaning in fiction. They show us his kind of self-conscious probing, and they show us his kind of affirmation of the human condition.

In the Preface to *The Twice-Told Tales*, Hawthorne speaks of "the coolness of a meditative habit, which diffuses itself through the feeling and observation of every sketch." [1] This "meditative habit" justifies Hawthorne's use of the distance of the romance.

1 *The Complete Works of Nathaniel Hawthorne*, Riverside Edition (Boston, 1883), I, 16.

The distance limits the reader's empathic attraction toward the characters and action and encourages the reader's involvement with Hawthorne's process of ordering his fictional elements. To the extent that we may speak of "empathy" in connection with Hawthorne's works, we probably should consider it functioning between the reader and the artist's mind in the process of "meditating" on the meaning of his works. We are very much aware of Hawthorne arranging his materials.

Both Hawthorne and his critics have likened this abstract quality to allegory. The comparison, however, can be misleading. In allegory the coordinates of meaning are fixed. The task of the reader is to locate his position at any given time in the narrative, according to these coordinates. In a complex allegory, such as *The Divine Comedy* or *The Faerie Queene*, several sets of coordinates may exist on different political or religious levels, but each set is static on its own level. With Hawthorne we are engaged more with a dynamic process of probing for meaning. Hawthorne may set forth a theme or idea, only to oppose it with its opposite, or he may consider a series of alternatives as a means to resolve a given theme. Usually we are as much aware of the process of weighing meanings as we are of any final solution.

We are also made very much aware of the artist's presence in this weighing of meanings. Hawthorne's sketch "Main Street" offers an illustrative condensation of his habitual self-consciousness as controlling artist. The tale concerns a pitchman who has fashioned a "pictorial exhibition" to show his audience the history of Salem's Main Street. He traces scenes from the "leaf-strewn forest-land" of the Indians and the "Eden" of the first settlers, to the coming of fences, the public shame of religious transgressors, the persecution of the Quakers, King Philip's War, and the trial of the Salem witches. In short, he develops a theme of progressive corruption. At six points, however, he is interrupted by an "acidulous-looking gentleman in blue glasses." This critic makes it a point "to see things precisely as they are," and directs attention to the fact that the pitchman's show is creaky artifice. He complains loudly, "Here is a pasteboard figure, such as a child would cut out

of a card, with a pair of very dull scissors; and the fellow mod-
estly requests us to see in it the prototype of hereditary beauty!" [2]
The critic plays *eiron* to the pitchman's *alazon*. The critic insists
that the spectators recognize they are receiving no more than a
piece of artifice arranged by the pitchman to carry meaning for
him. They are not receiving the past; they are receiving the pitchman's interpretation of the past. Invariably Hawthorne establishes
some equivalent to the critic's voice in his fiction to make us aware
of his presence as the artificer, or pitchman, arranging his materials. His candid assertion of himself in the process of probing for
meaning gives us a drama of the mind which is his own unique accomplishment with the romance form. It is a source of power for
him.

Before we can fully recognize Hawthorne's development of artifice in the romance form, however, we need some understanding of the basic world view with which we can expect to find him
dealing in his fiction. It seems to me that Hawthorne, although a
profoundly moral man, concerns himself much more with the
problem of man's relation to men than with man's relation to God
or to the universe. This idea is not startling. It is the position of
many, if not most, of Hawthorne's critics. Very convincingly the
position has been summed up by James K. Folsom in *Man's Accidents and God's Purposes*. Folsom sees Hawthorne in a Christian-
Platonic tradition which separates the world of God from the
world of men. Hawthorne's view "assumes two 'worlds,' that of
Man's accidents, which can be empirically known, and some ultimate Real world, that of God's purposes, which is inscrutable in
itself but upon which the former world depends." [3]

2 *Works*, III, 447.
3 Folsom, *Man's Accidents and God's Purposes: Multiplicity in Hawthorne's Fiction* (New Haven, 1963), pp. 13–14. Folsom shows the
pervasiveness of this attitude in Hawthorne's writings. He notes how
Hawthorne takes Melville to task, in his journal, for trying to "reason of
Providence and futurity, and of everything that lies beyond human
ken." And he quotes Hawthorne's comments on Confederate soldiers
taken prisoners, in "Chiefly about War Matters": "No human effort,
on a grand scale, has ever yet resulted according to the purpose of its
projectors. The advantages are always incidental. Man's accidents are
God's purposes."

Because of his belief in the inscrutableness of God's Providence, which he asserts over and over, Hawthorne directs most of his attention in his fiction to the knowable world of men. This world is often represented by what I take to be an ordering metaphor in Hawthorne's work—the image of life seen as a parade, a carnival, a spectacle, or a masquerade. This composite metaphor we may call a "procession of life," taking our term from Hawthorne's short story of that title. "Life figures itself to me as a festal or funereal procession," Hawthorne says in the first sentence of "The Procession of Life." His image as it develops in that story is of life as a parade toward death. The image is not unlike Pascal's metaphor of the human condition as men chained together like prisoners waiting to be executed one by one.[4] Both images have in common the idea that mortality is an overriding human bond. This idea appears also in Hawthorne's works in the procession of witches to the gallows in "Alice Doane's Appeal," in Oberon's dream of promenading on Broadway in a shroud in "Journal of a Solitary Man," and in the bridegroom's somber trick of turning the bridal procession into a funeral march in "The Wedding Knell."

But a reading of the metaphor of the procession as an embodiment of mortality would prove ultimately too reductive. We must remember that Hawthorne sees the procession as *festal* as well as *funereal*. Sometimes it is the great human energy of a festive gathering that Hawthorne chooses to emphasize. This he certainly does in his descriptions of the carnival in Rome in his *Italian Notebooks*. And human energy seems to be the most obvious facet of the procession in his major romances. The election-day parades in *The Scarlet Letter* and *The House of the Seven Gables* and the masquerade spectacles of *The Blithedale Romance* and *The Marble Faun* embody, more than anything else, great surges of human

4 Blaise Pascal, *Pensées et Opuscules* (Paris, 1957), p. 426. "Qu'on s'imagine un nombre d'hommes dans les chaînes, et tous condamnés à la mort, dont les uns étant chaque jour égorgés à la vue des autres, ceux qui resent voient leur propre condition dans celle de leurs semblables, et, se regardant les uns et les autres avec douleur et sans espérance, attendent à leur tour. C'est l'image de la condition des hommes."

activity. We need to see the metaphor on its broadest level as an image of man's world. At times Hawthorne may stress the mortality of that world, at other times its energy.

What is always present in the image is a sense of its plurality. The procession involves a sense of many diverse men held together in one unit. This is the crux of the image. For once this is established, Hawthorne can go on to work with the relationship of an outsider to the procession. No one would suggest that this relationship is Hawthorne's only theme, but it is an important one and one which is big enough to subsume many of Hawthorne's smaller themes. The relationship of the outsider to the unit of life is a subject Hawthorne never tired of examining. It dominates his moral and ethical views. It results in a doctrine of brotherhood.

The tales provide us with some clear examples both of Hawthorne's self-conscious probing for meaning and of his use of the procession of life. The self-conscious probing may be seen in "The Artist of the Beautiful," where Hawthorne speaks frequently in his own voice, and "Rappaccini's Daughter," where he uses a speculating protagonist in the action. The procession of life appears most prominently in "My Kinsman, Major Molineux," "Young Goodman Brown," "The Canterbury Pilgrims," and "The Maypole of Merry Mount."

In "The Artist of the Beautiful" Hawthorne speaks directly to the reader quite often. If we were to piece together Hawthorne's expository remarks, we would have before us a rather complete essay in defense of the artist's role in seeking beauty. These remarks, however, are set against a series of concrete scenes in the development of the career of his artist, Owen Warland, and elements in these scenes, along with a few of Hawthorne's own remarks, challenge Hawthorne's defense of his hero. The result is a dramatic tension between assertion and challenge that makes the reader aware he is engaged in an exploration for meaning, rather than a static illustration of fixed ideas. If we were to read the story as merely a step-by-step depiction of Owen's movement toward self-confidence, the story would be no more than a dull lecture with illustrative slides, but if we recognize such a movement set against a criticizing countermovement, then we can see the story correctly as a drama of the writer's mind as he painfully examines and seriously qualifies his defense of the artist.[5]

Owen Warland, in the tale, faces three "severe but inevitable" tests. They are his feelings about being of practical use, his longing for sympathy or understanding, and his desire for love. All three needs are denied him in his pursuit of beauty, and he must learn to overcome them to succeed as an artist.

At the beginning Owen is contrasted with the artisan, Robert Danforth. Peter Hovenden, the old watchmaker, and his daughter, Annie, watch both at their work. Seeing Danforth at his forge, Hovenden can appreciate the blacksmith's "main strength" and his products of iron. "He spends his labor upon a reality," Hovenden says. Owen, however, is bent over a "delicate piece of mechanism" which Hovenden thinks can be no more than a "Dutch toy." The watches and clocks in the window of Owen's watchmaker shop are turned from the street, "as if churlishly disinclined to inform the wayfarers what o'clock it was." And Hovenden tells us that Owen's skill only served in the past "to spoil the accuracy of some of the best watches in my shop." Owen is not interested in being useful. His aim, we quickly learn, is to capture beauty. As

5 Most of the critics have chosen sides. Two defend him as the Romantic artist unappreciated by mass man: Richard Harter Fogle, *Hawthorne's Fiction: The Light and the Dark* (Norman, Okla., 1952), pp. 70–90; and James W. Gargano, "Hawthorne's 'The Artist of the Beautiful,'" *American Literature*, XXXV (May, 1963), 225–230. Other critics, more interested in a psychological interpretation, see Owen Warland as a stunted man: Rudolph von Abele, *The Death of the Artist* (The Hague, 1955), pp. 32–44; William Bysshe Stein, "'The Artist of the Beautiful': Narcissus and the Thimble," *American Imago*, XVIII (Spring, 1961), 35–44; and Frederick C. Crews, *The Sins of the Fathers: Hawthorne's Psychological Themes* (New York, 1966), pp. 167–170. Most balanced is Millicent Bell, *Hawthorne's View of the Artist* (New York, 1962), pp. 94–113. She sees the tale as the Romantic view of the artist exaggerated to the point of a self-criticism. My reading differs from hers mainly in degree. I see Hawthorne finally endorsing his artist, but in a qualified way. She finds the self-criticism more overwhelming.

a child he wished to imitate, in wood carvings, the grace of birds in flight. Now he wants "to put the very spirit of beauty into form and give it motion." He is working on a mechanical butterfly that will be an "ideal," in the sense of a perfection of the shapes, colors, and movements of real butterflies.

Robert Danforth challenges the ethereal nature of Owen's work. "I put more main strength into one blow of my sledge hammer than all that you have expended since you were a 'prentice," Danforth tells him. Owen can answer that his "force" is of another kind, but Owen himself is not completely satisfied with the answer. Hawthorne, in his own voice, summarizes the test and offers his solution: "Thus it is that ideas, which grow up within the imagination and appear so lovely to it and of a value beyond whatever men call valuable, are exposed to be shattered and annihilated by contact with the practical. It is requisite for the ideal artist to possess a force of character that seems hardly compatible with its delicacy; he must keep his faith in himself while the incredulous world assails him with its utter disbelief...." [6] Owen does not have this kind of self-assurance at this stage in the tale, and so he sets to work as a watchmaker to please the practical wants of his fellow townsmen.

In the summer his dream returns when, like a child, he watches the movement of the butterflies and sees again a vision of perfect beauty. Working at night when no one can see him, he sets to work once more on his embodiment of the vision. But now he is aware of his isolation. He looks for sympathy and understanding to protect him from his loneliness. Annie's chance remark, a mocking gibe really, about "putting spirit into machinery," leads Owen to think she is capable of such sympathy. Hawthorne adds, "And what a help and strength would it be to him in his lonely toil if he could gain the sympathy of the only being he loved!" But before Owen can begin his explanation, Annie sees his creation, refers to it as a "little whirligig" and a "plaything for Queen Mab," and goes to set it in motion with the touch of a needle. This is enough. Owen sees that Annie cannot understand his goal. With a deeper

6 *Works*, II, 512.

sense of isolation, Owen uses his inheritance for drink and suffers a hallucinatory despair.

Again, however, his vision returns, and he goes back to his work at night. The third trial for him comes with the news that Annie will marry Robert Danforth. Not only are sympathy and understanding denied Owen, but also love. Hawthorne tells us somewhat jocularly, "Owen Warland's story would have been no tolerable representation of the troubled life of those who strive to create the beautiful, if, amid all other thwarting influences, love had not interposed to steal the cunning from his hand." [7] From the first, Owen considered his creation of an ideally beautiful work a means to win Annie's love, and Hawthorne indicates that in fact she did have a "woman's intuitive perception" of his love and of the creation he wanted to bring her. Seen in this light, her marriage to Danforth is a rejection of Owen's kind of subverted passion. He is left in total isolation to create his butterfly solely for his own appreciation of it. His reaction is to sink into a childish lethargy and to mock bizarre attempts in the past to "spiritualize machinery."

But he recovers from this test, as he did from the previous two, with the result that now he is strengthened. "Never did I feel such strength for it as now," Owen says when he resumes his work on the butterfly. He now recognizes that the artist must function with complete faith in his vision and his power to re-create it in art, despite the rejection of the people around him. He demonstrates this in the last scene when the child of Annie and Danforth destroys his creation. Owen's butterfly must be considered a success. Hawthorne says of it: "Nature's ideal butterfly was here realized in all its perfection." All three tests are recapitulated in the scene. Danforth attacks the butterfly's usefulness: "There is more real use in one downright blow of my sledge hammer." Annie "sympathizes" with her husband's remark and has for Owen "a secret scorn—too secret, perhaps, for her consciousness." Then in comparing Owen's butterfly, the creation of his kind of passion, with the child, the creation of her love with Danforth, Annie

7 *Ibid.,* p. 522.

clearly admires the child more. These three elements culminate in the child's destruction of the butterfly. This is an act of total rejection for Owen. But Hawthorne tells us Owen is now impervious: "When the artist rose high enough to achieve the beautiful; the symbol by which he made it perceptible to mortal senses became of little value in his eyes while his spirit possessed itself in the enjoyment of the reality." [8] The height of Owen's success came when he matched vision to creation. Society's acceptance or rejection of that moment cannot destroy the moment itself. Thus Hawthorne uses the story to trace out the strengthening of the artist's will to believe in himself.

But the story contains another level on which this achievement is questioned. What we have just described as a movement toward self-faith we could, from another view, describe as a movement toward self-delusion. Grounds for such a view are numerous.

Hawthorne himself raises the question whether the artist can ever match his vision perfectly to a concrete artifact. He declares: "Alas that the artist, whether in poetry, or whatever other material, may not content himself with the inward enjoyment of the beautiful, but must chase the flitting mystery beyond the verge of his ethereal domain, and crush its frail being in seizing it with a material grasp." [9] A comparison is implied between the crushed "flitting mystery" in the work of art and the butterfly destroyed by the child at the end. Both are, in their own degrees, destructions of the original vision. The work of art itself is suspect. Owen recognizes this when he admits to Annie that "this butterfly is not now to me what it was when I beheld it afar off in the daydreams of my youth." The admission is at first puzzling, for Hawthorne has already told us the "ideal butterfly was here realized in all its perfection," but the difficulty is resolved if we understand the butterfly to be a perfection of the type in nature, which, nevertheless, lacks the "flitting mystery" of abstraction now that it has physical substance. The point is that Hawthorne suggests the vision has been lowered by the creative act.

8 *Ibid.*, pp. 535–536.
9 *Ibid.*, p. 516.

If this is the case, we may well ask why the artist seeks to re-create his vision. This returns us to the question of usefulness. We should realize that the creation of a work of beauty need not be without any use. Idealists such as Emerson and Hegel insisted that the artist's rendering of the ideal could serve to awaken the perceptive powers of its viewers. They saw the work of art as the means by which the artist could communicate his vision to other people. Owen has this use in mind when he presents his butterfly to Annie and her family in the last scene. He tells her, "If you know how to value this gift, it can never come too late." But whatever traces of wonder he produces in Annie and Danforth, they are lost in the child's destructive act and Hovenden's "cold and scornful laugh." The last scene, while it demonstrates Owen's imperviousness, must also be considered an act of communication that fails. Without this communication, the artist is left with only the solipsistic knowledge that he has *almost* matched his vision with his skill. Hawthorne insists that we notice the narrowness of the achievement.

Hawthorne's notebook "germ" of the story stressed the uselessness of the creation: "To represent a man as spending life and intensest labor in the accomplishment of some mechanical trifle...."[10] Owen's butterfly is not such a trifle. We must take Hawthorne's word in the tale that Owen does capture an ideal beauty. But surely we are made aware, in the story, of Owen's infatuation for ingenious toys. Hawthorne states that in the past Owen has concocted such "freaks" as a "musical operation with the machinery of his watches," and Owen, in one of his lethargies, compares his butterfly to such hoaxes as Albertus Magnus' Man of Brass and Friar Bacon's Brazen Head and to such intricate toys as the automata of coach and horses made for a French king, a fly that buzzes, and a duck that waddles. There is in Owen, then, an absorption with ingenuity for its own sake, a preciousness.

10 *Passages from the American Notebooks* (Boston, 1868), I, 215. The development of this "germ" and its relationship to the other "mechanical trifles" in the tale have been traced by Ronald T. Curran in "Irony: Another Thematic Dimension to 'The Artist of the Beautiful,'" *Studies in Romanticism*, VI (Autumn, 1966), 34–45.

His motives for pursuing the ideal are also called squarely into account. It is one thing to search for beauty; it is another to cringe from the "main strength" of the practical world. Owen does as much of the latter as he does of the former. He appears as a ludicrous caricature of the sensitive artist in the vignette where, as a child, he is taken to see the steam engine: ". . . he turned pale and grew sick, as if something monstrous and unnatural had been presented to him. This horror was partly owing to the size and terrible energy of the iron laborer. . . ." [11] Similarly, Owen confesses that the "hard, brute force" of Danforth confuses him. The effect of the first meeting which we see is that Owen is so shaken he ruins his work. Also when Hovenden and Annie pass by his shop, his nerves "flutter" and his heart "throbs" so much that he cannot work. Most revealing of all, though, is the fact already noted that Owen can seek Annie's love only on the subverted level of preparing his butterfly for her. He refuses to think of her as a woman. He sees her instead as an embodiment of ideal beauty. This, Hawthorne tells us emphatically, is wrong. In the practical world Owen is too sensitive. His fragility is always before us. Every piece of his physical description emphasizes it. His face is "pale" and it has "small features"; his "ears are as delicate as his feelings"; his frame is "diminuative" or "small and slender"; his voice, "low and slender"; his hand, "delicate" and "little"; his brain, "sensitive"; he "quivers," "shrinks," and can "scarcely lift his head" in the presence of the other characters. Hawthorne pictures Owen as an overly sensitive person in fear of the practical world. Art offers him the escape of complete withdrawal.

Finally, though, it is Owen's isolation we must consider. At the end of the story he can communicate with no one. If the townspeople cannot hurt him, neither can he affect them. It is interesting that at each test which Owen endures he sinks to a lower level of despair. While this despair hardens him, it may also indicate his growing fear of aloneness. Against the child of Annie and Danforth, all Owen can offer is the butterfly which the child easily crushes. His only strength is his self-assurance that he is an artist,

11 *Works*, II, 507.

and even in this he is a little like the madman who believes he is Napoleon, with no one else to confirm his judgment.

The narrowness of what Owen has accomplished, the escapist nature of his absorption, and the isolation inherent in his role are all factors which Hawthorne uses to qualify his defense of Owen. They are fearful prices required for the creative moment. What we are most aware of in this tale is Hawthorne's process of balancing attributes as he works toward his highly qualified, severely challenged endorsement of the artist.

"Rappaccini's Daughter" is somewhat different. Essentially this tale is the initiation into experience of Giovanni Guasconti, the student newly arrived in Padua, who encounters the mysteries of Rappaccini's garden and Rappaccini's daughter, Beatrice. Giovanni is a speculator on meaning within the action of the story. However, Hawthorne also enters the story in his own voice, as *eiron* this time, to question the integrity of Giovanni. He tells us of Giovanni in the midst of his investigation of Beatrice: "Guasconti had not a deep heart—or, at all events, its depths were not sounded now; but he had a quick fancy, and an ardent southern temperament, which rose every instant to a higher fever pitch." [12] And before Giovanni submits Beatrice to a final "decisive test," Hawthorne comments on Giovanni's looking into a mirror: "a vanity to be expected in a beautiful young man, yet, as displaying itself at that troubled and feverish moment, the token of a certain shallowness of feeling and insincerity of character." [13] Hawthorne questions the validity of some of the evidence Giovanni compiles. Giovanni thinks he sees drops of moisture from a flower Beatrice picks kill a lizard; he thinks he sees an insect die when it comes too near her; and he thinks he sees flowers he has thrown Beatrice fade in her arms. Hawthorne reminds us that Giovanni has had much to drink and that his ability to see such details from his window is doubtful. Later Giovanni is vindicated, when Beatrice confesses the poison in her system, but the scene does force the reader to recognize Giovanni's point of view as not infallible. Similarly,

12 *Ibid.*, p. 122.
13 *Ibid.*, p. 140.

Hawthorne reminds us that Giovanni listens to the explanations of Baglioni without knowing that Baglioni is an intense rival to Rappaccini in the world of science. By presenting a speculator and then questioning his findings, Hawthorne directs our attention to the process of speculation itself in the tale. We follow not just Giovanni's mind, but also a more generalized, disembodied conception of a mind at work, which includes a critical sense of Giovanni's fallibility—the mind of the artist behind the story.

The mysteries Giovanni confronts have to do with the bewilderingly contradictory quality of the human condition. Both the garden and Beatrice embody this contradictory quality. At first appearance the garden is a mixture of natural growth and human art: "Every portion of the soil was peopled with plants and herbs.... Some were placed in urns, rich with old carving, and others in common garden pots; some crept serpent-like along the ground or climbed on high, using whatever means of ascent was offered them. One plant had wreathed itself round a statue of Vertumnus...." [14] The impression of the scene is one of contention between nature and human art. The impression of contention deepens for Giovanni as he watches Rappaccini move among the plants with the demeanor of "one walking among malignant influences, such as savage beasts, or deadly snakes, or evil spirits, which, should he allow them one moment of license, would wreak upon him some terrible fatality." While this initial impression of contention proves to be correct, the emphasis on the power of nature over human skill soon becomes reversed. When Giovanni actually enters the garden he finds that it is Rappaccini who has done violence to the natural order. The artificially cross-pollinated plants seem to him "unnatural," a "commixture, and, as it were, adultery, of various vegetable species," and perhaps even "the monstrous offspring of man's depraved fancy." Through his skill, Rappaccini has apparently perverted natural order to create a garden of poison. Yet Giovanni cannot be sure that what Rappaccini has done is a perversion, for Rappaccini's aim is to experiment with vaccines, an aim in which Giovanni detects a "noble

14 *Ibid.*, p. 111.

spirit." Like life itself, the garden is thus a complex blend of natural processes and human contrivances.

As guides to us in our speculation on the tale's mysteries, if not to Giovanni, Hawthorne offers the two symbols of the spring and the shrub. They are opposites. They emphasize the work's ordering artifice, and they mark off the extreme boundaries of our probing. The water of the spring rushes from a shattered and ruined marble fountain, reflecting light. Giovanni feels "as if the fountain were an immortal spirit that sung its song unceasingly and without heeding the vicissitudes around it, while one century imbodied it in marble and another scattered the perishable garniture on the soil." [15] The spring is an emblem of natural purity which continues to exist amid the decay or corruption of man-made contrivances. Opposed to it is the lush purple shrub, "so resplendent that it seemed enough to illuminate the garden." Like the fountain, it appears to be a source of beauty and light, but the shrub is nature perverted to a deadly toxic plant by Rappaccini. As Beatrice tells Giovanni, it has been "created" by her father, and it is "fatal." It is emblematic of natural purity despoiled by human contrivance. Both of these symbols reflect aspects of Beatrice.

At first sight, Giovanni notices a visual analogy between the "rich flower and beautiful girl." The shrub is closely associated with Beatrice. She tends the plant when her father dares not. She embraces it sensually and breathes in its heavy perfume. "Give me thy breath, my sister," she cries. When Giovanni asks about the origin of the plant, she confesses that Rappaccini created it on the day she was born and that she has grown up nourished by its poisonous fragrance. She, like the plant, has been made into a vehicle of poison through the machinations of Rappaccini.

The precise aspect of evil this poison represents is not totally clear. Probably Hawthorne does not intend it to be particularized. Yet we can see it as rooted in the drive for power of the two scientists, Rappaccini and Baglioni. Both pervert natural life in order to achieve a prideful position of control. In this respect, the last picture of Rappaccini is very revealing: "As he drew near, the pale

15 *Ibid.*, p. 111.

man of science seemed to gaze with a triumphant expression at the
beautiful youth and maiden, as might an artist who should spend
his life in achieving a picture or a group of statuary and finally be
satisfied with his success. He paused; his bent form grew erect
with conscious power; he spread out his hands over them...." [16]
Baglioni exhibits the same pose of "conscious power" in the last
lines of the tale, when he gloats over his defeat of Rappaccini's
plan. Certainly the motives of both have good intentions inter-
mixed—as we said earlier of Rappaccini's motives in "perverting"
the garden—but the net effect of their manipulations is that they
isolate Beatrice and Giovanni from the natural flow of life which
both want to participate in. Beatrice herself is guilty, unintentionally, of the same crime when she infuses her poison into Giovanni
and, in effect, makes him a prisoner in the garden.

However, innocence also exists in Beatrice. When Giovanni
meets her for the first time, she insists she has no understanding of
her father's science. "Forget whatever you may have fancied in
regard to me. If true to the outward senses, still it may be false in
its essence," she tells Giovanni, indicating the possibility of an innocence beneath any outward semblance of corruption. She admits that the unnaturalness of some of the flowers shocks her as
much as it does him. Cut off from the world outside the garden,
she is untouched by worldly knowledge. She talks "about matters
as simple as the daylight or summer clouds." In conversation with
him "Her spirit gushed out before him like a fresh rill that was
just catching its first glimpse of the sunlight," and her thoughts
and dreams "sparkled upward among the bubbles of the foun-
tains." In short, Giovanni finds a sense of uncorrupted purity in
Beatrice analogous to the purity of the fountain, despite the cor-
ruptions of her father's garden.

The tale itself involves the process of the mind vacillating between these extreme possibilities, trying to understand the contradictory aspect of the human condition they describe.[17] As we

16 *Ibid.*, p. 146.
17 I see Beatrice as the commixture of good and evil in human experience.
   Most other critics have tried to limit her meaning more narrowly. Roy

follow Giovanni's fallible speculations, we seek to reconcile our-
selves to human experience, where corruption and innocence in-
termingle. After his initial attraction to Beatrice and to the garden
seen from his window, Giovanni learns from Baglioni of the dangerous aspect of Rappaccini's experiments. Then, watching Beatrice again, Giovanni thinks he receives the three pieces of evidence mentioned earlier that show her to be a source of poison.
At this point Giovanni experiences a "lurid intermixture" of love
and horror, and also thinks he finds in Beatrice's gaze "the mystery
of which he deemed the riddle of his own existence." In other
words, Giovanni is face to face with life on its most complex level.
Were he to accept this complexity, his education would be ful-
filled. But rather than accepting Beatrice's complexity, he fastens
on her innocence as they talk: "Whatever had looked ugly was
now beautiful; or, if incapable of such a change, it stole away and
hid itself among those shapeless half ideas which throng the dim
region beyond the daylight of our perfect consciousness." [18] Baglioni begins Giovanni's next reversal with his warning that Rappaccini is experimenting on Giovanni and his story of the poisonous
maiden sent to Alexander the Great. These warnings are substan-
tiated by three new pieces of evidence Giovanni gathers, which
this time are irrefutable: flowers wilt in his hand; his breath kills a

---

Male, *Hawthorne's Tragic Vision* (Austin, Tex., 1957), pp. 54–70, finds
her a source of spiritual regeneration. Oliver Evans, "Allegory and Incest
in 'Rappaccini's Daughter,'" *Nineteenth-Century Fiction*, XIX (September, 1964), 185–195, defines her as Eve. Frederick Crews, *The Sins of
the Fathers*, pp. 117–135, calls her the embodiment of erotic love. And
Norman A. Anderson, "'Rappaccini's Daughter': A Keatsian Analogue?"
PMLA, LXXXIII (May, 1968), 271–283, compares her to the vision of
the imagination in "Lamia." Each of these interpretations has its validity
on a certain level, but finally Beatrice must be grasped as a more com-
prehensive symbol. Two critics who have taken her this way are Hyatt
H. Waggoner and Sidney P. Moss. For Waggoner, Beatrice is fallen
humanity, and for Moss, she represents an ambiguity that can only be
approached by a series of propositions concerning good and evil. See
Waggoner, *Hawthorne: A Critical Study* (Cambridge, Mass., 1955),
pp. 101–107; and Moss, "A Reading of 'Rappaccini's Daughter,'" *Studies
in Short Fiction*, II (Winter, 1965), 145–156.
18 *Works*, II, 132–133.

spider; and as a demonstration before Beatrice, he kills a swarm of insects with his breath. But when he attacks Beatrice for what she has done to him, she insists on her innocence by denying that she intended to harm him. The events of the past seem to bear her out, for she stopped him from approaching the purple shrub, and she repelled him when he came too close to her. Giovanni has no reason to doubt her when she exclaims, "I dreamed only to love thee and be with thee a little time, and so to let thee pass away, leaving but thine image in mine heart; for, Giovanni, believe it, though my body be nourished with poison, my spirit is God's creature, and craves love as its daily food." [19] She stands before him unmistakable in both her innocence and corruption. Giovanni is initiated: "There now came across him a sense, mournful, and not without tenderness, of the intimate and peculiar relationship between Beatrice and himself." [20]

There is no solution to the complexity Giovanni finds, only an understanding of it. To stay with Beatrice as she is would be to exist in unnatural isolation. This is impossible anyway, Hawthorne states, because Giovanni's bitter attack on Beatrice has hurt her too much. Giovanni turns to the potion of Baglioni as a desperate means to regain innocence, but only sinks deeper into corruption, for now he, like Beatrice before, unintentionally poisons the other. The complex aspect of human experience is inescapable. We follow the mind's progress in this tale as it works toward knowledge of that incontrovertible fact. Giovanni's speculations, with Hawthorne's criticism of them and the artifice of his organizing symbols of the shrub and the spring, make the tale a drama of the mind searching for meaning. Our attention is directed more at the searching than it is at the resultant meaning. It is interesting to note that Hawthorne himself, in writing the story, was not sure whether Beatrice was "angel or demon." [21] The story is finally Hawthorne's self-conscious probing of the intermixture of both.

19 *Ibid.*, pp. 144–145.
20 *Ibid.*, p. 145.
21 Julian Hawthorne, *Nathaniel Hawthorne and His Wife* (Boston, 1884), I, 360.

The relationship of the outsider to the procession of life is a situation so recurrent that we may think of it as an archetype in Hawthorne's work. Usually the procession, festal or funereal, represents a kind of complexity similar to what we found in Beatrice, and it is the outsider's task to comprehend its complexity and even affirm it and enter it. An inquiry into *why* Hawthorne found this relationship of the outsider to the procession so important would take us way beyond the scope of this book. We would probably discover its roots in Hawthorne's introverted personality rather than in a consciously reasoned moral doctrine of brotherhood: in Hawthorne's understanding of the need to break through the barrier of restrictive self-preoccupation into free, open, and continuous communication with other men, an understanding resulting from his own failure to accomplish this except in bits and flashes. Yet this hypothesis, I must admit, would be difficult, if not impossible, to prove, because Hawthorne's personality and his moral vision are so intimately tied together. Frederick Crews, in *The Sins of the Fathers*, gives primacy to Hawthorne's repressive personality over any concept of a reasoned moral stand, in attempting to explain Hawthorne's creative process. While his explanation seems the most valid offered thus far, Crews is able to arrive at it as easily as he does only because he accepts almost arbitrarily Freud's concept of the id-driven man over Freud's later concept of the ego-controlled man. Another critic, Roy Male, in an article on Hawthorne's use of the word *sympathy*, argues that Hawthorne's doctrine of brotherhood has its foundations in nineteenth-century science.[22] Chemic, electric, and magnetic experiments in attraction and repulsion, Male insists, provided Hawthorne with a rationally arrived-at conception of the interrelation of all things. Undeniably science furnished Hawthorne much of his most striking imagery (as, for example, Hester, Dimmesdale, and Pearl as an "electric chain" in the middle scaffold scene of *The Scarlet Letter*), but as a source for Hawthorne's fascination with the relationship of the one to the many, science is unconvincing.

22 Male, "Hawthorne and the Concept of Sympathy," *PMLA*, LXVIII (March, 1953), 138–149.

If we are to consider rationally adopted stances, surely the New Testament concepts of the brotherhood of man, which Hawthorne would have found in the Unitarianism of his family, would be a much more likely place to begin. But I propose to sidestep the question of whether Hawthorne's introverted personality shaped his moral vision or whether a consciously hammered-out moral vision dominated his personality. That is a problem for a different kind of study. Suffice it here to state that Hawthorne did have an engrossing interest in the relationship of the individual to the procession of life. His examinations of the relationship usually raised both moral and psychological problems, and Hawthorne was deeply concerned with both.

Whether the problems were moral, psychological, or both, Hawthorne always insisted that the individual must come to affirm a tie with the procession of life, must come to achieve some sense of the brotherhood of men. This despite the fact that the brotherhood of men could be, in a large measure, repellent. Such is the case in Hawthorne's short stories of initiation, "My Kinsman, Major Molineux" and "Young Goodman Brown." The first seems to me largely a psychological study and the second a moral study.

Robin, the protagonist of "My Kinsman, Major Molineux," comes to the town as an eighteen-year-old innocent from the country. The object of his quest is, from the first, contradictory. He leaves home to make his way in the world, but his method for trying to do this is to find Major Molineux, a guardian cousin, who would protect him. (The French root of the name suggests a softness, and hence perhaps a protectiveness.) On the one hand, Robin wants to enter into adult experience, but on the other, he fears to give up the protectiveness inherent in boyhood. Enter adult life he does, however. His entry into the town is a baptism into the complexity of adult experience.[23] Once he enters, the simple, sure as-

23 I follow here the general tendency of a school of critics who read the story as a dreamlike search by an innocent adolescent for maturity through the overthrowing of restrictive authority. The school of critics includes: Simon O. Lesser, "The Image of the Father," *Partisan Review*, XXII (Summer, 1955), 372–390; Franklin B. Newman, "My Kinsman, Major Molineaux [sic]," *University of Kansas City Review*, XXI (March,

pects of life seen by a boy are denied him forever. He comes to
hoot and jeer, with the crowd of patriots, his once powerful kinsman, and to accept tacitly the guidance of the gentleman who tells
him, "perhaps, as you are a shrewd youth, you may rise in the
world without the help of your kinsman, Major Molineux."

What is unusual about this tale of initiation is that the complexity of adult experience is presented in virtually the worst possible
light. Robin's experience in the town frustrates, bewilders, and
angers him. The tempo of mocking laughter increases around
Robin, and important action, time and time again, seems out of
sight around a corner from him.[24] The first man Robin meets, the
gentleman with the two sepulchral hems, brushes aside his questions with the apparent *non sequitur*, "I have authority." The inn-
keeper accuses Robin of being a fugitive. The lady with the scarlet
petticoats tries to seduce him. And the man with double promi-
nences on his forehead promises that Robin shall find his kinsman
if he waits an hour on the church steps late at night. All these
puzzles in response to his questions about his kinsman. Thus Robin
encounters what to him must be a nightmare of confusion.[25] All

---

1955), 203–212; Hyatt H. Waggoner, *Hawthorne: A Critical Study*,
pp. 46–53; Seymour L. Gross, "Hawthorne's 'My Kinsman, Major Molineux': History as Moral Adventure," *Nineteenth-Century Fiction*, XII
(September, 1957), 97–109; Louis Paul, "A Psychoanalytic Reading of
Hawthorne's 'Major Molineux,'" *American Imago*, XVIII (Fall, 1961),
279–288; and Frederick C. Crews, *The Sins of the Fathers*, pp. 72–79.
Another group of critics sees the story as an allegory of the American
urge for independence. Undoubtedly they are correct as far as they go,
but their point is ultimately trivial. What is interesting in this story is
how Hawthorne embodies that allegory in the initiation experience of the
youth from the country. This second group includes: Q. D. Leavis,
"Hawthorne as Poet, I," *Sewanee Review*, LIX (Spring, 1951), 179–205;
Roy Harvey Pearce, "Hawthorne and the Sense of the Past, or the Im-
mortality of Major Molineux," *Journal of English Literary History*, XXI
(December, 1954), 327–349; and John Russell, "Allegory and 'My Kinsman, Major Molineux,'" *New England Quarterly*, XL (September,
1967), 432–440.

24 The first point is made by Waggoner, in *Hawthorne: A Critical Study*,
pp. 47–50, and the second by Newman, in "My Kinsman," p. 207.

25 This, of course, is much more true for Robin than it is for us. With his
historical introduction on colonial revolt Hawthorne has provided us

the figures seem threatening to him. Worst, perhaps, is the watch-man with his spiked staff, who orders him off the streets and does not even hear or will not reply to Robin's question about Major Molineux. For comfort, Robin, who is the son of a minister, looks into a church through its window. But he is assailed more by the emptiness of the church than anything else. His thoughts then revert to a scene at his home in the country, where he dreams of his father reading the Bible to his family beneath the great tree by the house, but the figures in his dream went into the house, "the latch tinkled into its place, and he was excluded from his home." Feeling himself totally alone, cut off from the world of his youth and caught in a world that he cannot understand, Robin loses his sense of reality. The mansion with a Gothic window across the street from the church changes shapes. Its pillars become trees and then people. Robin sees a face which we later learn is that of the man of the two hems, and Robin thinks it resembles Molineux's. He has moved from a simple, ordered life in the country to a chaotic nightmare world.

This nightmare confusion is exactly what is summed up by the procession which Robin encounters:

> A mighty stream of people now emptied into the street, and came rolling slowly towards the church. A single horseman wheeled the corner in the midst of them, and close behind him came a band of fearful wind-instruments, sending forth a fresher discord now that no intervening buildings kept it from the ear. Then a redder light disturbed the moonbeams, and a dense multitude of torches shone along the street, concealing, by their glare, whatever object they illuminated. The single horseman, clad in a military dress, and bear-ing a drawn sword, rode onward as the leader, and, by his fierce and variegated countenance, appeared like war personified; the red of one cheek was an emblem of fire and sword; the blackness of the other betokened the mourning that attends them. In his train were wild figures in the Indian dress, and many fantastic shapes without a model, giving the whole march a visionary air, as if a dream had

with a plausible explanation for the behavior of the townspeople and has given us a comic vantage point on Robin's confusion. But at the same time Hawthorne records Robin's reactions fully enough so that we can share his confusion even while we see through it.

broken forth from some feverish brain, and were sweeping visibly
through the midnight streets. A mass of people, inactive, except as
applauding spectators, hemmed the procession in; and several women
ran along the sidewalk, piercing the confusion of heavier sounds
with their shrill voices of mirth or terror.[26]

Every sentence stresses a confusion and antiphony in the procession. It is a violent contrast to the peaceful scene Robin has left
behind in the country. Yet Robin is drawn deeper and deeper into
the atmosphere of this procession until he laughs the loudest of all
at his tarred and feathered kinsman. There are many reasons for
his laughter. First, he is caught up in the "bewildering excitement"
of the crowd. Second, the scene offers him a release from the
anxiety of not knowing what is happening around him. Third,
Molineux provides Robin with a scapegoat against whom Robin
can turn the kind of laughter directed at himself earlier. Fourth,
the tarring and feathering puts an end to any hope Robin had of
continuing to live under a guardian, a situation calling for violent
emotional response, and given the first three factors, laughter
would supply this kind of release. But more important than the
reasons why Robin laughs is the fact that he *does* laugh, that is, the
fact that he joins the townspeople in their attack on Molineux. We
can only see this attack as cruel. If Molineux has been despotic, we
have no knowledge of his despotism. We see only "the foul dis-
grace of a head grown gray in honor." Thus when Robin joins the
patriots emotionally, we sense he is joining a harsh, cruel group.
And Hawthorne specifically reinforces our reaction by his own
denunciation of the procession: "On they went, in counterfeited
pomp, in senseless uproar, in frenzied merriment, trampling all on
an old man's heart. On swept the tumult, and left a silent street behind." [27] There is no indication that Robin ought to avoid joining
the procession; there is no indication even that he could avoid
joining the procession. But Hawthorne makes us see the cost of his
joining. Robin has to give up a secure, ordered, and innocent
world when he enters adulthood. Upon entering he becomes liable

26 *Works*, III, 637–638.
27 *Ibid.*, p. 640.

to a fearsome array of complex emotions. That fearsomeness is
what Hawthorne chooses to emphasize.

"Young Goodman Brown" is a moral analogue to "My Kinsman, Major Molineux." It deals with much the same subject matter. At the outset we are told Brown has been married to his wife
Faith for only three months. Hawthorne labels him a novice. The
implications are twofold. Allegorically, we may consider him new
to the realization of a faith. He is a young good man, but he has
not thought out his faith fully, nor has he tested it against human
experience. He proposes to leave Faith behind, safe in his house,
while he joins the devil's rites in the forest, with the rationaliza-
tion that the following morning he will return to his faith, "cling
to her skirts and follow her to heaven." Brown's faith depends on
a neat separation of saintliness and sinfulness. On the naturalistic
level, however, his recent marriage suggests an initiation into adult
experience and hence an approaching end to his innocent conception of faith.[28] He is a novice in both faith and experience. We
can expect a collision.

Like Robin, Goodman Brown seeks out his initiation on a
journey into a night world. Brown goes into the hallucinatory
forest as Robin went into the nightmare town. An important difference, however, is that Brown knows the "evil purpose" of his
journey. He is much more conscious of the moral dilemma of his
quest. Consequently he proceeds hesitatingly. Although he has
undertaken the journey of his own free will, he argues with himself and with the devil about turning back. With his simplistic
conception of a world of saints and sinners, Brown feels he had
better remain with the saints. But subtly the devil attacks Brown's
idea of the saints. He testifies to the evil of Brown's father and
grandfather, shows him the woman who taught him his catechism
as a witch, allows him to overhear phantoms of the minister and
the deacon on their way to the rites in the forest, and at last ar-

28 See E. Arthur Robinson, "The Vision of Goodman Brown: A Source
and Interpretation," *American Literature*, XXXV (May, 1963), 222.
Robinson makes much the same point: "The implication is that Brown's
marital experience has awakened him to recognition of the universal role
of sex, with special relevance to sin."

ranges for him to hear Faith, perhaps lamenting, perhaps entreating, also on her way to the rites.

At this juncture, with his concept of faith destroyed, Goodman Brown goes to the ceremony and confronts the procession. It is terrifying in its confusion of the orders Brown had previously held separate:

> Either the sudden gleams of light flashing over the obscure field bedazzled Goodman Brown, or he recognized a score of church members of Salem village famous for their especial sanctity. Good old Deacon Gookin had arrived, and waited at the skirts of that venerable saint, his revered pastor. But, irreverently consorting with these grave, reputable, and pious people, these elders of the church, these chaste dames and dewy virgins, there were men of dissolute lives and women of spotted fame, wretches given over to all mean and filthy vice, and suspected even of horrid crimes. It was strange to see that the good shrank not from the wicked, nor were the sinners abashed by the saints. Scattered also among their pale-faced enemies were the Indian priests, or powwows, who had often scared their native forest with more hideous incantations than any known to English witchcraft.[29]

Toward this procession Brown feels a "loathful brotherhood by the sympathy of all that was wicked in his heart." Brown looks on the human capacity for evil. The devil urges him toward a new simplistic conception of man. "Evil is the nature of mankind," he tells Brown. Brown and his Faith stand, "the only pair, as it seemed, who were yet hesitating on the verge of wickedness in this dark world." Then Brown chooses the worst alternative open to him. He refuses to accept the initiation into the procession. He clings, in other words, to his notion of saintliness separated from sinfulness.[30] He will not admit to man's capacity to sin. Had he

29 *Works*, II, 101.
30 This position has been worked out at length in different ways by Roy Male, *Hawthorne's Tragic Vision*, pp. 76–80, and Joseph T. McCullen, "'Young Goodman Brown': Presumption and Despair," *Discourse*, II (July, 1959), 145–157. Male writes of Brown's need for "a perspective broad enough and deep enough to see the dark night as an essential part of human experience, but a part that may prelude a new and richer dawn." McCullen attacks Brown as a moral "absolutist." He quotes Hawthorne's statement in "Fancy's Show Box" on moral complexity:

entered the procession, he might have perished. But he might also have pushed through to a sympathetic understanding of man's complex capacities for both good and evil. Goody Cloyse does instruct children well, we may assume from her long service in that role, and the townspeople find the minister and the deacon admirable leaders. Faith wants to be a loving wife. But Brown, having seen their dark capacities, refuses to acknowledge any other capacities. As a result, he cuts himself off from the brotherhood of men. It can be argued that he is hypocritical to cut himself off from the procession, for Hawthorne has told us that Brown did have a "sympathy" toward it by "all that was wicked in his heart." We may also assume that there was a latent capacity for evil in Brown which prompted his visit to the forest in the first place. By clinging hypocritically to a simplistic morality, Brown loses his chance to enter humanity.

Robin joins the procession in "My Kinsman, Major Molineux," and Brown pulls back from it in "Young Goodman Brown." We do not know whether Robin's entry will be beneficial or harmful; we only know that it is necessary for him if he wishes to grow from the simple, innocent world of childhood. He at least avoids the fate of Goodman Brown, who clings stubbornly to his concept of innocence despite evidence of a more complex world. Goodman Brown's empty life serves as a kind of justification for Robin's entry into the procession, hard and discordant as the procession is. Hawthorne offers this sort of negative argument over and over again. One must affirm life, hard and sin-laden though it may be sometimes, because the alternative, isolation, offers no hope at all. He uses this argument, for instance, in "The Christmas Banquet." The story concerns, we remember, a Christmas banquet set for the ten most miserable persons whom the trustees of a certain estate can find. A guest they invite year after year is Gervayse Hastings, who appears to all the town to be one of its most successful citizens. The other guests, who change from year

"In truth, there is no such thing in man's nature as settled and full resolve, either for good or evil, except at the very moment of execution" (*Works*, I, 257).

to year, wonder at his presence until finally Gervayse explains his misery. His explanation comes in response to the death of one of the guests. " 'Would that he could teach me somewhat!' said Gervayse Hastings, drawing a long breath. 'Men pass before me like shadows on the wall; their actions, passions, feelings, are flickerings of the light, and then they vanish!' " [31] His misery stems from his isolation. He is unable to sense the actions, passions, and feelings of other men as real, and so he is cut off from life. "Neither have I myself any real existence," he says, "but am a shadow like the rest." [32] So too Hawthorne's men of intellect in his tales—Ethan Brand, Aylmer, and Rappaccini—cut themselves off from a sympathetic bond with the brotherhood of men in order to undertake what was for Hawthorne "the unpardonable sin" of experimenting on other human beings. The agony of their isolation, like Gervayse Hastings', is argument enough for Hawthorne to urge commitment to the brotherhood of men even at its worst.[33]

More positively Hawthorne writes, in stories such as "The Canterbury Pilgrims" and "The Maypole of Merry Mount," about an admirable courage of those who freely elect to test themselves against the severity of the procession of life. Of course any fool can enter life unknowingly, naively. (Robin has proved that.) The role of hero Hawthorne reserves for those who join the procession with complete knowledge of its difficulties. These heroes are willing to accept the challenge of human complexity.

In "The Canterbury Pilgrims," Josiah and Miriam, two innocents from a Shaker community, are on the verge of leaving the protective colony to go into the world at large where they will be free to marry. They meet a procession of "pilgrims" who are fleeing life. The first two, a poet and a merchant, tell the lovers about their disappointments in their quest for fame and wealth. Then speak a married couple who, like Josiah and Miriam, wanted only

31 *Works*, II, 337–338.
32 *Ibid.*, p. 345.
33 This argument is spelled out in no uncertain terms in "Ethan Brand," where the procession of idlers who seek Brand out comes close to representing the brotherhood of men at its most ineffectual. Nonetheless, Brand condemns himself for his separation from them.

to earn a living and nourish their love. The husband tells of his failure at work, and the wife tells of the gradual decay of their love. "Your love will wear away by little and little," the wife tells Miriam, "and leave you miserable at last. It has been so with us; and yet my husband and I were true lovers once, if ever two young folks were." [34] The pilgrims present to Josiah and Miriam a "dark array of cares and sorrows." But the lovers go on into the world, Hawthorne tells us, "with chastened hopes, but more confiding affections." The implication is that the lovers have a fuller understanding of their love as means of sustaining themselves in life than they had at the beginning of the tale.

These implications are developed further and more clearly in "The Maypole of Merry Mount." The young couple of this tale, Edgar and Edith, begin in the midst of one kind of procession and then move into another. They are to be wed as part of the May celebration at Merry Mount. The first procession is a presentation of sensual delight outside a moral sphere.

> On the shoulders of a comely youth uprose the head and branching antlers of a stag; a second, human in all other points, had the grim visage of a wolf; a third, still with the trunk and limbs of a mortal man, showed the beard and horns of a venerable he-goat. There was the likeness of a bear erect, brute in all but his hind legs, which were adorned with pink silk stockings. And here again, almost as wondrous, stood a real bear of the dark forest, lending each of his fore paws to the grasp of a human hand, and as ready for the dance as any in that circle.[35]

The animal looks like the people, and the people resemble animals. The revelers of Merry Mount, like Donatello in *The Marble Faun*, are innocent in the sense of being subhuman. They know only the delights of a purely sensual world of nature. They do not know the complexities of the human world.

Edgar and Edith sense that this is so when they marry. In pledging themselves to each other, they realize that they are undertaking a complex human tie. Hawthorne puts it this way: "No

34 *Works*, III, 529.
35 *Works*, I, 71.

sooner had their hearts glowed with real passion than they were sensible of something vague and unsubstantial in their former pleasures, and felt a dreary presentiment of inevitable change. From the moment that they truly loved, they had subjected themselves to earth's doom of care and sorrow, and troubled joy, and had no more a home at Merry Mount." [36] The harsh aspects of life are immediately presented to the lovers in the form of the new spectacle they must confront.

> The ring of gay masquers was disordered and broken; the stag lowered his antlers in dismay; the wolf grew weaker than a lamb; the bells of the morris-dancers tinkled with tremulous affright. The Puritans had played a characteristic part in the Maypole mummeries. Their darksome figures were intermixed with the wild shapes of their foes, and made the scene a picture of the moment, when waking thoughts start up amid the scattered fantasies of a dream. The leader of the hostile party stood in the centre of the circle, while the route of monsters cowered around him, like evil spirits in the presence of a dread magician. No fantastic foolery could look him in the face. So stern was the energy of his aspect, that the whole man, visage, frame, and soul, seemed wrought of iron, gifted with life and thought, yet all of one substance with his headpiece and breastplate.[37]

In their spectacle, the sensualism of the revelers has come under the domination of the Puritans, who serve as an embodiment of an ordered social and moral world, typically for Hawthorne shown at its most extreme. The response of the lovers is to come to each other's defense. Each asks to take the punishment of the other. In doing this, Edgar and Edith exhibit a willingness to accept their responsibility for each other, or to put it yet another way, they demonstrate the validity of their marriage tie. This link between the two individuals is the first, and probably most important, step into the human brotherhood.

The Puritans recognize the strength of the tie of Edgar and Edith, and so while they cut Edgar's hair and put more modest clothes on the lovers, they grant them a garland of flowers, "so,

36 *Ibid.*, p. 75.
37 *Ibid.*, p. 79.

in the tie that united them, were intertwined all the purest and best of their early joys." The garland is the final symbol of the tale. It fuses the meanings of the two worlds. It holds together the joy of the revelers and the sense of ordered ties between people of the Puritans.

Edgar and Edith go into the world, as Hawthorne says, "supporting each other along the difficult path which it was their lot to tread." The modern reader could react to this ending with mutterings about sunsets, violins, and sentimentalism.[38] And perhaps rightly so. Almost any writer when he speaks positively of endorsing life lays himself open to charges of sentimentalism. But Hawthorne's defense is that Edgar and Edith are genuinely heroic, because they have looked at the grimmest aspect of the social order and are still willing to join it. By marrying they entered a kind of social order. Their entry into the world is an exploration of the consequences of that act on a larger scale.

Up to this point we have considered the metaphor of the procession to represent a human brotherhood sometimes vital and sometimes harsh. We need to notice another aspect. Often the metaphor entails a certain amount of illusoriness. This is most obvious when the processions are presented in dumb shows, as is the case with the procession of history in "Main Street" and with the scenes of history displayed by the showman in "Ethan Brand," or when the processions are spectacles, like the balls in "Howe's Masquerade" and "Lady Eleanore's Mantle." Yet this quality exists also in the processions faced by Robin, Brown, and Edgar and Edith. The life they confront has an illusory quality. The Puritans in their armor, in "The Maypole of Merry Mount," are as "cos-

---

38 Frederick C. Crews, *The Sins of the Fathers*, pp. 17–25, has mounted such an attack. He finds the moral doctrine banal, but feels the story becomes more interesting when seen as a conflict of Puritanism and hedonism. The moral situation is, I think, somewhat more complex than he is willing to admit, and the conflict of Puritanism versus hedonism more banal, at least to post-Freudian readers, than he states. Yet the really important point which should be made about this story is that the moral framework and the psychological framework are absolutely compatible. Hawthorne is working here with Freud's balance of pleasure principle and reality principle, but he is using his own terms, pleasure and care.

tumed" as the revelers. Both worlds have illusory aspects. In "Young Goodman Brown" the hallucination in the forest points up for Brown the possibility that the townspeople are only masquerading as saints during the day. And Robin's procession is actually presented to us as something that might have been dreamed.

The implication of this is enormous. Hawthorne suggests tacitly that life itself may be illusory, "the shadow of a dream." Yet if it is, his characters must still affirm it, for it is the only world they as mortals have. A character such as Gervayse Hastings, who sees life only as a dream, robs himself of existence. The suggestion of illusoriness is, of course, consistent with Hawthorne's Christian-Platonism, which posits a higher reality above the world of men. But still the idea of illusoriness, suggested so often by Hawthorne, is one further reason why Hawthorne should accept the act of entering life as one calling for courage. None of the characters we have been examining so far, except Gervayse, understands this illusory aspect of the world they face. Yet it is there. And we should see it as being there, making their confrontation that much more difficult.

My argument in this chapter has been twofold. I contend that Hawthorne uses the quality of artifice basic to the romance form to focus attention on his probing for meaning. He calls attention to his own presence as the mind in the act of weighing and evaluating the action of the work. Thus, while he places the action of the work at a distance from the reader, he brings the drama of the artist's mind very close indeed to his audience. I also contend that the problem Hawthorne investigates over and over again, in the romance form, is the individual's affirmation of life with other mortal men. The procession of life is always complex, but the individual, if he is to grow rather than wither, must enter this complexity. With these two propositions in mind, we may now look at his four major romances to see the artifice Hawthorne uses to probe his concern for the affirmation of the mortal condition.

Part two

The four major romances

Chapter III

The Scarlet Letter:
"A tale of human frailty
and sorrow"

In *The Scarlet Letter* Hawthorne approaches the problem of the individual and the human predicament in terms of the Puritan experience. His object is to set clear the dilemma without sacrificing a sense of its human complexity. His aim is not unlimited ambiguity, as one critic has maintained,[1] for his complexity has its defining boundaries, similar to those we found in "Rappaccini's

---

1 F. O. Matthiessen, *American Renaissance: Art and Expression in the Age of Emerson and Whitman* (New York, 1941), pp. 275–282. Matthiessen coins the phrase "the device of multiple choice" as explanation of Hawthorne's technique in *The Scarlet Letter*.

Daughter." Nor is it to produce the richness of many levels of symbolic meaning, as another implies,[2] for *The Scarlet Letter* contains only a single level of interpretation beneath the literal. Neither the term *allegory* nor *symbolism* will suffice for the combination of simplicity and richness that stamps *The Scarlet Letter* a masterpiece. Instead, we must go to Hawthorne's assumptions of the romance form. What we find in *The Scarlet Letter* is a human dilemma, stripped of its irrelevancies and removed to the distance of romance abstraction so that Hawthorne may self-consciously probe its range of possible consequences.

The Scarlet Letter begins as a standard New England romance. In the first four chapters Hawthorne presents the conventional opposition of the black Puritan and the fair Puritan.[3] So emblematic are these figures that they establish the work's level of conscious artifice at once. They force us to see *The Scarlet Letter* as a work concerned with the process of analyzing, rather than reproducing, human experience. These two figures define the extreme positions of the book's ethical and moral argument. While readers of Hawthorne may well differ—and have in fact differed widely [4]—on which of Hawthorne's solutions to emphasize, they ought to agree on the forces pitted against each other in the work. For readers to agree on this would be no slight thing. It would indicate that we can see the outlines of the argument, and it would imply that we can proceed on our way toward penetrating the

2 Hyatt H. Waggoner, *Hawthorne: A Critical Study* (Cambridge, Mass., 1955), pp. 118–150.

3 A marked tendency of recent criticism is to veer away from a moral interpretation of *The Scarlet Letter*. For example, Frederick C. Crews, *The Sins of the Fathers: Hawthorne's Psychological Themes* (New York, 1966), pp. 136–153, finds the power of the book in its revelation of certain psychological states of repression, and Ernest Sandeen, "*The Scarlet Letter* as a Love Story," *PMLA*, LXXVII (September, 1962), 425–435, thinks it depends on the treatment of a tragic love. Both critics have valid points to make. But I want to argue here that the focus is the moral dilemma. To this dilemma, of course, Hawthorne's treatments of psychological states and of tragic love may be seen to contribute mightily.

4 For a sampling of the range of opinion, see Charles C. Walcutt, "*The Scarlet Letter* and Its Modern Critics," *Nineteenth-Century Fiction*, VII (March, 1953), 251–264.

texture of the argument, toward entering Hawthorne's process of weighing alternative consequences to the dilemma he puts in front of us.

As the romance begins, we are quickly made aware that the setting is not just a physical place, but also a moral landscape. We encounter an expanding series of opposing images.[5] First our attention focuses on a prison door. It is dark, severe, and ugly. Hawthorne associates it with the civilized world that constructed it. It represents the harshness of society's laws. Beside it grows a wild rose bush, a representative of the unrestricted world of nature, in obvious contrast to the prison door. The rose bush is delicate and fragile. It seems to offer its beauty to the prisoner "in token that the deep heart of Nature could pity and be kind."

This contrasting set of images is developed in human terms in the next chapter. The Puritan women of "The Market-Place" are extensions of the prison. They are manlike in their aggressiveness and severity. One woman—called an "autumnal matron"—wants Hester branded on the forehead for her adultery, and another, described as "the ugliest as well as the most pitiless of the self-constituted judges," calls out, "This woman has brought shame upon us all, and ought to die. Is there no law for it?" In contrast to this grim chorus of matrons is the softly feminine young wife holding her child by the hand. She understands Hester's anguish and feels sympathy for her. "O, peace, neighbours, peace!" she whispers. "Do not let her hear you! Not a stitch in that embroidered letter, but she has felt it in her heart." [6] We should note that the young wife stresses the word *heart*. We first encountered it in connection with the rose bush as a token of the "heart of nature." The heart will, of course, become a dominant image in the book when we see Dimmesdale continually covering his heart with his hand. For the moment, let it suffice to say that Hawthorne uses the heart as a metaphor in the standard nineteenth-century way as the seat

5 The initial opposition of the prison and the rose bush is noticed by many critics, most importantly by Richard Fogle, *Hawthorne's Fiction: The Light and the Dark* (Norman, Okla., 1952), pp. 14, 104–105, and Waggoner, *Hawthorne: A Critical Study*, pp. 119–120.
6 *The Scarlet Letter*, Centenary Edition (Columbus, 1962), p. 54.

of the emotions. The young wife opposed to the matrons illustrates the natural emotions as against severe social laws of behavior. But we cannot say the matrons represent the *head*, seat of reason in the standard dichotomy Hawthorne was fond of speculating on in his notebooks. The matrons in their pursuit of fulfilling the letter of the law go far beyond any sense of reasoned justice. They are as emotionally charged in their defense of the law as the young wife is in her sympathy.

In precisely this context are Hester and Chillingworth presented to us. They are part of the series of opposed images. Hester is almost literally an intensification of the young wife. She carries her child in her arms. The striking richness of her attire and her dark hair make her woman on the large scale. Hawthorne likens her to the madonna of Renaissance art. Her role as representative of unrestricted, natural emotions is made all the more clear by contrast with the beadle marching before her as an embodiment of "the whole dismal severity of the Puritan code of law." The role of the beadle is quickly subsumed by Chillingworth. Seeing himself as an aging husband who wronged Hester by bringing her to a loveless marriage, he can forgive her adultery as no more than a counterbalancing wrong. But he burns to make the escaped lover suffer. Here he becomes Hester's ultimate adversary. In his demoniacal drive, he embodies the severest aspects of the hard justice of the Puritans to which Hester stands irrevocably opposed.

The opening movement of *The Scarlet Letter*, then, unfolds in a series of contrasts that define the boundaries of opposition in the work. The series may be diagrammed for convenience this way:

Ethical and moral conflict

Prison versus *Rose Bush*
(emblem of society's restrictive laws)   *(unrestricted nature)*

Puritan Matrons versus *Young Wife with Child*
(severe, manlike purveyors of society's laws)   *(feminine woman of natural, unrestricted emotion of sympathy)*

Beadle versus *Hester with Pearl*
(emblem of severity   *(woman guilty of sin*
of society's laws)   *of unrestricted emotion)*

Chillingworth versus *Hester*
(severe purveyor of   *(woman guilty of sin*
society's laws)   *of unrestricted emotion)*

The conflict reduced to its simplest terms exists between the laws of behavior fundamental to an ordered, moral society and the ungoverned, natural emotions of the human heart. With the dark-visaged Chillingworth and the feminine, loving Hester representing the two forces, we see that Hawthorne confronts us with the conventional opposition of the black Puritan and the fair Puritan. Hawthorne even shares the bias of contemporary romancers, initially at least, in showing Puritan severity in the worst and Hester's loving nature in the best possible light (as for instance in her loyalty to Dimmesdale on the pillory). But Hester differs from her prototype. Visually she is dark rather than blond. Ethically she is guilty of a demonstrable social wrong. From the beginning the simple opposition suggests future complexities beyond the conventional. Similarly, the neatness of the dichotomy must be suspect, for as we have seen, the purveyors of the social law are not without their *emotion*, which might be termed *natural* and *unrestricted* as well as the young wife's and Hester's. Yet despite these objections, or warnings of future complications, it is the clear-cut extremities of the conflict that Hawthorne wants us to recognize at the outset of *The Scarlet Letter*. By means of the partial abstractions of the fair Puritan and the black Puritan, he establishes the limits of the dilemma he is going to treat. They define the area to be probed and call attention to the work's artifice. The conventional opposition launches Hawthorne.

Directly between the two forces stands Arthur Dimmesdale. He is the romance's most complex character, its most "real" character, for he encompasses in his personality both of the extremes

Hester and Chillingworth define.[7] He has participated in the unrestricted passion of Hester, and he has punished himself as severely as even Chillingworth could require. A certain psychological complexity is apparent in him from the first speech he makes
to Hester on the scaffold. He commands her to name her lover, *if*,
and *only if*, he implies, naming him will aid her salvation and
bring peace to her soul. Since naming her lover can do no more
than reduce Hester's period for wearing the letter, Dimmesdale is
effectively asking her not to reveal him. As he continues his
speech, however, he contradicts himself. Hester's silence can only
tempt her lover to "add hypocrisy to sin," he reasons. Ironically,
Hester has been the fortunate one. Heaven has marked her guilt
with the child Pearl. Ought she to withhold the similar relief of
identification from her lover, he asks. Now he is on the verge of
asking her, truly, to do what he is too weak to do—reveal his sin.
He wants to confess, and he does not want to confess. This is exactly his state of mind when he ascends the scaffold late at night
and calls out neither long enough nor loud enough to be discovered, when he sermonizes on his imperfection, knowing his parish-
ioners will not believe him, and when he allows Chillingworth to
probe him with his cat-and-mouse tactics. Dimmesdale has committed what he and his society feel to be a sin of unrestricted emotion. The need to redeem himself weighs heavily on him. Public
confession is the means he envisions.

That his confession needs to be public is a vexing problem.[8] It

7 One of the amusing aspects of Hawthorne criticism is the way critics
   have fought over the notion of whose book *The Scarlet Letter* is,
   Hester's or Dimmesdale's. Indeed, most of the dozens of the most recent
   articles are concerned with defending a camp. I would want to urge a
   return to a "relativistic" reading such as that undertaken by John C.
   Gerber, "Form and Content in *The Scarlet Letter*," *New England Quarterly*, XVII (March, 1944), 25–55, where we study the effect each has on
   the other. While I consider Dimmesdale to be easily the most "complex"
   character in *The Scarlet Letter*, I do not necessarily call the book "his."
8 In particular, it vexes Edward Davidson, "Dimmesdale's Fall," *New
   England Quarterly*, XXXVI (September, 1963), 358–370, and William
   Nolte, "Hawthorne's Dimmesdale: A Small Man Gone Wrong," *New
   England Quarterly*, XXXVIII (June, 1965), 168–186, both of whom find
   the confession a kind of bribe for grace.

smacks of tawdry exhibitionism. Why can't Dimmesdale repent his moral sin to God in private and tacitly balance his social offense by good works, we might well ask. Of course, the most immediate answer must be that a public confession is irrevocable, whereas a private confession to God may be countermanded at will. Also, in psychological terms, public confession would be the most excruciating form of masochism open to Dimmesdale if we assume, as Frederick Crews suggests, that Dimmesdale has repressed his sexual drive and converted it through reaction formation to self-flagellation.[9] Then, too, public confession would remove the stain of hypocrisy from Dimmesdale. All of these answers seem valid for Dimmesdale the man. But for Dimmesdale the character, in a world view ordered by Hawthorne the artificer, we must go back to the fundamental idea of all of Hawthorne's fiction, the idea that the individual must affirm sympathetic ties with his fellow human beings, sin-stained though they may be. Public confession is for Dimmesdale an affirmation that he is one with his fellow mortals.

Hawthorne discusses Dimmesdale's need to affirm his common humanity largely through the imagery of the heart. Dimmesdale's need is to affirm that he has a human heart, capable of human emotions both good and evil. In a crucial passage on Dimmesdale's religiousness, Hawthorne speculates that if Dimmesdale had not sinned, he would have belonged to a class of saintly men perfect in all respects save that they lacked the "tongue of flame," which Hawthorne interprets as the power of "addressing the whole human brotherhood in the heart's native language." [10] The passage is particularly telling because Hawthorne hastens to add that Dimmesdale's sermons had grown in power since his act of adultery. The burden of the sin, Hawthorne states, "gave him sympathies so intimate with the sinful brotherhood of mankind; so that his *heart* vibrated in unison with theirs, and received their pain

9 Crews, *The Sins of the Fathers*, pp. 136–153.
10 This passage has been brilliantly discussed by Roy Male in "The Tongue of Flame: *The Scarlet Letter*," *Hawthorne's Tragic Vision* (Austin, Tex., 1957), pp. 90–118. I have drawn heavily on his reading here.

into itself, and sent its own throb of pain through a thousand other *hearts,* in gushes of sad, persuasive eloquence" (p. 142, italics mine). Because Dimmesdale has acted with Hester according to the emotion of his imperfect heart, he has open to him the gift of speaking with the "tongue of flame"—"Heaven's last and rarest attestation" of the office of spiritual leaders. Yet he fails to recognize this positive aspect of his sin. In the forest with Hester, he berates himself because he allows his congregation to listen to him "as if a tongue of Pentecost were speaking." He feels he is unworthy to speak with the Pentecostal "tongue of flame" because he is a sinner, when ironically Hawthorne has already established that a knowledge of sin is necessary for total spiritual communication. Dimmesdale can see only the destructive aspects of his sin.

The situation confronting Dimmesdale is also treated by means of emblematic characters such as we saw established at the beginning of the book. Chillingworth continues to represent a severe purging force. His immediate effect on Dimmesdale is debilitating. Chillingworth keeps Dimmesdale alive only to prolong the tortuous game Chillingworth enjoys playing with the minister. Yet we need not be concerned with Chillingworth's motivation at the moment. Here we may consider him an externalized force in what is essentially Dimmesdale's own psychodrama. When Chillingworth is not present, we know from the bloody scourge that Dimmesdale himself plays Chillingworth's part. Indeed, it is easy to imagine Dimmesdale alone in the famous interrogation scene of "The Leech and His Patient" playing both the role of prosecutor and of defendant, presenting himself with the black roots from the dead man's heart, and putting Chillingworth's questions to himself in the hope that he can refute them. The ease with which Dimmesdale turns aside Chillingworth's first group of questions indicates that Dimmesdale has been over the questions before in his own mind. The scene is a dramatization of what Hawthorne calls Dimmesdale's "constant introspection wherewith he tortured, but could not purify, himself" (p. 145). Even Chillingworth's final thrust, which confounds Dimmesdale and ends the questioning at that point, is only an elaboration of Dimmesdale's plea on the scaffold to Hester to save him from hypocrisy. Chillingworth rejects Dimmesdale's claim that some men maintain the false appearance of innocence in order to have the opportunity to perform good works. "These men deceive themselves," answers Chillingworth. "They fear to take up the shame that rightfully belongs to them. Their love for man, their zeal for God's service,—these holy impulses may or may not coexist in their hearts with the evil inmates to which their guilt has unbarred the door, and which must needs propagate a hellish breed within them. But, if they seek to glorify God, let them not lift heavenward their unclean hands! If they would serve their fellow-men, let them do it by making manifest the power and reality of conscience, in constraining them to penitential self-abasement!" (p. 133). Chillingworth puts it nicely. Ironically, he almost brings Dimmesdale to the means for escaping his torture—public confession.[11] But Chillingworth knows his man, in this instance. Dimmesdale is not able to confess yet, and so the torture may go on, draining Dimmesdale of his energy and his will to enter the human world. Chillingworth goads Dimmesdale toward destruction by playing on his self-loathing, his horror at the base stains in himself. These Chillingworth holds up before him.

The life-giving aspects of Dimmesdale's sin are represented by Pearl. Surely an unconvincing human character, she is, nevertheless, a very important and very complicated symbolic one. Literally she is the result of Dimmesdale's sin. Hawthorne refers to her as the "living hieroglyphic" of the sin. Dressed in scarlet, she is an embodiment of the letter *A*. For Dimmesdale to acknowledge her, of course, is another way for Dimmesdale to confess his guilt. So on a naturalistic level her very existence implies a means of escape from Chillingworth's hold. (Indeed, Dimmesdale feared a hereditary resemblance might give him away.) The biblical connotations of her name—usually associated with purity attained through Christ or baptism—and Hawthorne's phrase describing her as worthy of Eden suggest that she stands for the human heart

11 One psychoanalytical critic likens Chillingworth's performance to a psychoanalyst using a "talk cure." See Eugene Arden, "Hawthorne's 'Case of Arthur D.,'" *American Imago*, XVIII (Spring, 1961), 45–55.

purified or the state of grace. We do see her in this role at the brookside, when she stands separated by the stream from Dimmesdale and wreathed in flowers, almost a medieval icon for grace, a pearl maiden. But this is not her most prominent role. Mainly she is a humanizing or life-giving force for Dimmesdale. This role is best illustrated during the middle scaffold scene, when Dimmesdale partially claims her by taking her hand and being joined by her to Hester during the night. "The minister felt for the child's other hand, and took it. The moment that he did so, there came what seemed a tumultuous rush of new life, other life than his own, pouring like a torrent into his heart, and hurrying through all his veins, as if the mother and the child were communicating their vital warmth to his half-torpid system. The three formed an electric chain" (p. 153). Taking Pearl's hand is perhaps an image contrasted to Dimmesdale's usual pose of covering his heart with his hand. The vignette on the pillory is strikingly like Hawthorne's usual representations of the human condition in its emphasis on energy. Dimmesdale feels a tremendous inflow of energy from this movement toward the release of confession. This is the end which Pearl chiefly signifies. She represents the strength-giving powers of the human heart. Therefore, we may extend our original diagram to describe Dimmesdale's conflict in this way:

Chillingworth,	*Dimmesdale*	*Hester,*
the Black Puritan		*the Fair Puritan*
(severe restrictions on social conduct)	*(the sinner)*	*(unrestricted human emotions)*
Chillingworth	*Dimmesdale*	*Pearl*
(debilitating force through loathing of unrestricted human emotions)	*(the sinner)*	*(life-giving force through affirmation of human emotions)*

The second step above grows logically out of the first. In order for Dimmesdale to gain self-knowledge and an understanding of other men, he must recognize that he has human emotions. Then he may enter into a sympathetic understanding of his fellow men.

To do this he must affirm Pearl. That done, he may feel the rush of energy of being part of a vital life force. But at the same time Dimmesdale knows and never doubts that he has committed a social and moral wrong. Therefore he wishes to purge himself of the tendency to sin. This is another way of saying that Dimmesdale is blocked in gaining self-knowledge because he loathes what he must affirm. Like Hamlet, he shrinks back from the contamination of the world in which he has to act.

As was the case with the opposing forces we found at the beginning, the roles of Chillingworth and Pearl overlap. The diagram should only serve to hold them apart momentarily. Pearl, for example, is in her own way just as torturing as Chillingworth. When the physician probes Dimmesdale with his questions in their lodging, Pearl comes to the window not to save Dimmesdale but to add her taunts. The cruelty of the daughter strongly affects Dimmesdale. In his dreams he is haunted by the figure of Pearl pointing her forefinger first at Hester's letter and then at Dimmesdale's own breast. The dream gesture is repeated twice more in the flow of real events.[12] On the scaffold at night, Pearl points to the dark form of Chillingworth watching the scene, and in the forest she points at her mother's breast, now stripped of the letter. In both instances she reminds Dimmesdale of the torturing aspect of the sin. Similarly, she heightens his agony by asking on the scaffold and in the forest when will he take her hand in front of the other people of Boston. We may say that these acts will eventually be regenerative for Dimmesdale since they push him toward realization of his flawed human condition. Yet if we say this of Pearl's role, must we not say it of Chillingworth's? Certainly Dimmesdale comes to feel before his death that the torture inflicted by Chillingworth has served ultimately a positive function in the design of Providence. He thanks God for an avenger to keep

12 See Anne Marie McNamara, "The Character of Flame: The Function of Pearl," *American Literature*, XXVII (January, 1956), 537–553. McNamara makes this point and examines at length Pearl's role as goad to Dimmesdale. However, she goes too far when she claims Pearl is the "motivation" for Dimmesdale's confession. I would prefer to put it that Pearl symbolizes the positive force which drives him to confession.

the torture "always at red-heat." The answer to our question must
be *yes.* Chillingworth ultimately serves a positive function too.

Dimmesdale is guilty of the sin of intellectual pride as well as
the sin of adultery.[13] This pride is what gives Chillingworth his
hold, for as long as Dimmesdale refuses to admit his sin to his fellow citizens Chillingworth can terrorize him with the prospect of
his being found out. Dimmesdale's pride is Satan's sin. It cuts
Dimmesdale off from his fellow human beings, and it defines him
as one trying to rival God. The man who will be more than mortal is guilty of what was to Hawthorne the "unpardonable sin."
We can produce a clutch of short stories such as "Egotism; or,
The Bosom Serpent" and "Lady Eleanore's Mantle" to support
the idea that Hawthorne often attacked such sinners. But readers
of Hawthorne's works know perfectly well that he can feel, on
occasion, some admiration for the strength and drive of prideful
characters. In *The Scarlet Letter* the force of Dimmesdale's pride
which Chillingworth's tortures intensify is absolutely essential to
his final regeneration.[14]

Hawthorne's attitudes toward the pride of two characters in his
tales, Ethan Brand and Aylmer, will clarify his attitude toward
Dimmesdale. Brand, it will be remembered, leaves his lime kiln to
try to seek out the "unpardonable sin." He travels the world looking into the hearts of other human beings to find their worst passion. Finally he learns that the unpardonable sin is his own sin of
intellectual pride in using the souls of others merely to satisfy his
morbid curiosity. Hawthorne states in one of his notebooks that
Brand's kind of sin consisted "in a want of love and reverence for
the Human Soul; in consequence of which, the investigator pried
into its dark depths, not with the hope or purpose of making it
better, but from a cold philosophical curiosity—content that it

13 This guilt is convincingly stressed by Davidson in "Dimmesdale's Fall."
14 Cf. Donald A. Ringe, "Hawthorne's Psychology of the Head and Heart,"
   PMLA, LXV (March, 1950), 120–132. Ringe makes the point that
   through a balance of emotions and intellect the Hawthornean character
   may achieve an anonymous well-being, but for a character to reach
   heroic stature he must dare the sin of too much intellect.

should be wicked in whatever kind or degree, and only desiring to study it out." [15] The sin results from a transformation in Brand during his search. At the outset his motives were more admirable. He remembers that he started the quest with "love and sympathy for mankind" and "pity for human guilt." But as he pursued his goal, he developed his intellectual powers at the expense of losing his sympathetic ties with fellow human beings. Brand comes to see himself as a prideful figure looking down on other men as specimens in his experiment. Yet it is interesting that Brand in some ways is more appealing than the buffoons of the town who cluster around him. While his pride has pushed him away from all human feeling, it has also pushed him to an understanding of the human predicament that none of the townspeople, except the child Joe, is capable of grasping.

Aylmer, too, violates the human heart through an act of pride in "The Birthmark." He administers a potion to his wife in order to remove her birthmark, the one stain on her otherwise perfect face. He knows full well the danger of his experiment. Yet he continues it in his lust to create a perfectly beautiful human being. He strives for too much. The perfection he wants is beyond the human sphere. So in his pride he brings his wife to her death. However, we must respect Aylmer's longing to create a work of perfect beauty. If we fail to do so, we miss the tension of the story. Aylmer's longing to make a human being perfect is the very essence of western humanism. True, Aylmer goes too far in pursuing his vision, but the vision itself is a noble one. We realize Aylmer is wrong to play God, but we admire the drive to remove the stain of imperfection from the human form.

Dimmesdale resembles both these prideful heroes. Like Aylmer he has a longing that is noble as well as prideful, and like Brand he gains a kind of self-knowledge denied to others through the pride that separates him from others. At the beginning of the work, Dimmesdale wishes to deny the existence of sinful emotions in his heart. His act of adultery has shown him that they do, in

15 *The American Notebooks by Nathaniel Hawthorne*, ed. Randall Stewart (New Haven, 1932), p. 106.

fact, exist there, but he wishes to see the adultery as an aberration he can rectify. He cannot confess publicly, or totally to himself, because he refuses to believe that the capacity to sin is fundamental to his human condition. Therefore he scourges himself and submits to Chillingworth's interrogations to purify himself. His refusal to accept the capacity to sin is directly contrary to Hawthorne's notion that the individual must see the world as it is in order to act in it. But the refusal has a nobility. It is founded on Dimmesdale's desperately held longing to rise to the highest level of human life, to move toward perfection, and to strive toward his God.

The true nature of his condition is revealed to him in the forest with Hester. After seven years of trying to purge himself of his longing for Hester, Dimmesdale encounters her alone and discovers that his emotion is exactly as it was. Now he is forced to admit to himself that such emotions are fundamental to his nature. No amount of penitence can drive them out. He recognizes his common mortality. The result is a flow of energy through his body, more intense and lasting than the energy he felt on the scaffold at night. Dimmesdale describes his feeling to Hester: "I seem to have flung myself—sick, sin-stained, and sorrow-blackened—down upon these forest-leaves, and to have risen up all made anew, and with new powers to glorify Him that hath been merciful! This is already the better life!" (pp. 201–202). He feels a release from his self-torture in this new affirmation of the emotions of his heart.

But while such emotions may be freely indulged in the forest, the world of nature, they must be restricted and governed in the world of men. This Dimmesdale discovers during the six confrontations he has on his walk back to town. In the first five cases, he is tempted to follow his emotions, but recognizes a need to curb them. He is tempted to make blasphemous suggestions about the Last Supper to a deacon, destroy a lonely old woman's belief in an afterlife, make lecherous signs to a young virgin, tell dirty words to a group of children, and trade off-color jokes with a drunken sailor. Each emotion Dimmesdale finds either needlessly harmful to other human beings or degradingly self-indulgent. What he has done in affirming his emotions becomes clear when he meets Mistress Hibbins in the sixth confrontation. He has, in effect, given his soul momentarily to the Black Man of the Forest. That is, he has consigned himself to the pursuit of emotions that may often be evil. Importantly, Hawthorne puts this revelation mostly in ethical rather than moral terms. If Dimmesdale were to follow his emotions completely, he would, quite demonstrably, hurt other human beings.

Dimmesdale now enters his third phase. He admits the full range of his human heart and seeks to atone for its base aspects. The shift from his initial situation is subtle. By the end of the work, he rejects both of the extreme positions open to him at the start and moves toward a synthesis. First, he rejects the debilitating aspects of severe punishment by cutting off Chillingworth's attempts to question him after his return from the forest. In doing this Dimmesdale strikes the pose of synthesis, as Anne Marie McNamara has shown us,[16] by standing with one hand on the Hebrew scriptures (severe justice) and the other on his heart (unrestricted emotion). Second, at some point between his return to the town and the delivery of his election sermon, he rejects Hester's plan to run off to follow their emotions completely. The intellectual pride of Dimmesdale, so obviously a negative aspect of Dimmesdale earlier, now saves him from a life of utter self-indulgence. With his new knowledge he can recognize his heart for what it is and enter the brotherhood of men; but he refuses to sink into a brutish indulgence of his heart; he still wishes to rise to the highest level of life and to lead his fellow men with him. This is pride in the best sense, for it is coupled with humble recognition of the evil of which he is capable.

Seen from this perspective, the final pillory scene is a moment of triumph for Dimmesdale. At the election sermon, Dimmesdale speaks out with the "tongue of flame" on the relationship between the human condition and the divine. Hawthorne describes the effect of his voice: "Like all other music, it breathed passion and

16 *Op. cit.*, p. 549.

pathos, and emotions high or tender, in a tongue native to the human heart, wherever educated" (p. 243). Dimmesdale can now speak fully in the heart's native tongue, because he recognizes the full range of his own heart. At the same time, however, he urges his audience not to despair of attaining the grace of God. The overriding effect of his sermon is the note of hope that comes from the "passion and pathos" in his voice. The confession that follows outside the meeting house is a dramatic re-enactment of the sermon. Dimmesdale confesses his sin and throws himself repentant before God with hope. His act is a message to the other sin-tainted mortals around him. His final moment is one of leadership. Here on the scaffold he claims Pearl and escapes Chillingworth's destruction.

The question of whether or not Dimmesdale has received grace cannot be answered. The answer lies beyond the scope of the book. All we can say is that he has done everything in his power to understand his human condition, to repent its base aspects, and to lead his fellow mortals well. By any human standards he has acquitted himself as nobly as possible, but divine grace is beyond his human comprehension. So when Hester asks if they will be together in an afterlife, he can give no definitive answer. He fears and he hopes. All we may see at the end of the work are the two separate graves with the single tombstone to answer our own wondering. What we may conclude positively about Dimmesdale is that he has brought himself to the point where grace may come to him, and this is the most positive statement we should expect from Hawthorne. Dimmesdale is as triumphant as a *human being* can be.

Hester follows a similar pattern, but with the difference that she lacks Dimmesdale's driving pride and his intellectual ability. She is almost completely a woman of feeling and emotion. From the very beginning she is prepared to accept her imperfect heart as Dimmesdale is not. Her difficulty comes in trying to adjust to society's reasoned classification of her. Society's laws have

branded her an adultress.[17] What does that mean to her? She has
had certain emotions. That is all she knows. Should she atone for
her emotions or leave Boston to find a place where she may follow
her emotions freely? Early in the book she accepts society's judgment that she needs to atone. However, we know she does not totally accept the judgment, because in the forest she proposes to
Dimmesdale that they flee together, in other words, that they
leave behind society's abstract concepts of good and bad, purity
and sin, to commit themselves to their feelings. Hester cannot
make up her mind. Starting strong, she becomes more and more
vacillating (and probably more and more interesting to the
reader).

Like Dimmesdale, Hester is caught between two forces. For
her, both are represented in Pearl. Dimmesdale spells out Pearl's
dual role at Bellingham's mansion when the officials consider taking Pearl from Hester: "This child of its father's guilt and its
mother's shame hath come from the hand of God, to work in
many ways upon her heart, who pleads so earnestly, and with such
bitterness of spirit, the right to keep her. It was meant for a blessing; for the one blessing of her life! It was meant, doubtless, as the
mother herself hath told us, for a retribution too; a torture, to be
felt at many an unthought of moment; a pang, a sting, an ever-
recurring agony, in the midst of a troubled joy!" (p. 114). Pearl
is a daughter on whom Hester can pour all her love and emotion,
but Pearl is also a reminder of the sin Hester has committed. Hester, then, may be shown also in a diagram as the center of the conflict as well as one of its extremes.

17 Two critical points of view have opened on this situation. Frederick I.
Carpenter, "Scarlet A Minus," *College English*, V (January, 1944), 173–
180, asserts that Hester finds her own truth in her independence. And
Darrel Abel, "Hawthorne's Hester," *College English*, XIII (March,
1952), 303–309, maintains that Hester loses her vitality in isolation. Both
views are, I think, too extreme. Hester does find a role for herself which
allows her to continue living without cracking under the strain of her
isolation. This we must admire. But at the same time we must admit that
she does not achieve any consciousness of her human condition that
could raise her to a heroic level.

Pearl	Hester	Pearl
(torturous	*(the sinner)*	*(source of life*
reminder		*as someone*
of the sin)		*to be loved)*

Where Hester differs from Dimmesdale in such a diagram is in
her lack of ability to reconcile the two forces. She remains always
the victim of divergent pulls.

At one point, when Hester looks at one of the Puritan matrons,
she cannot believe that the ice in the matron's heart makes the matron superior to her. Hawthorne says she *struggled* to believe her
emotions were sinful, as the townspeople would have her believe.
The struggle costs her the femininity that was almost her definition when we first saw her.

> It was a sad transformation, too, that her rich and luxuriant hair had
> either been cut off, or was so completely hidden by a cap, that not
> a shining lock of it ever once gushed into the sunshine. It was due in
> part to all these causes, but still more to something else, that there
> seemed to be no longer any thing in Hester's face for Love to dwell
> upon; nothing in Hester's form, though majestic and statue-like,
> that Passion would ever dream of clasping in its embrace; nothing
> in Hester's bosom, to make it ever again the pillow of Affection.
> Some attribute had departed from her, the permanence of which
> had been essential to keep her a woman [p. 163].

Much of the reason for her change, Hawthorne tells us, is that her
life had changed from passion and feeling to thought. The result
of her thought, her intellectual pondering of her situation, is, un-
fortunately, the repression of what is good in her. Here she is an
exact contrast to Dimmesdale. He could see the need to restrain
his base emotions. She feels compelled to restrain *all* her emotions.
And all her emotions which we actually see in the work are quite
admirable and beneficial to her society.

Hester gains little knowledge from her conflict. Hawthorne
tells us that she fancied the scarlet letter "gave her a sympathetic
knowledge of the hidden sin in other hearts" (p. 86), but she refuses, or is unable, to act on this glimpse of truth as Dimmesdale
does. She can momentarily regain her femininity in the forest by

throwing off her letter, but she cannot progress beyond that stage. When Dimmesdale makes his confession and turns to her with the question, "Is not this better . . . than what we dreamed of in the forest?" she can only answer, baffled, "I know not! I know not!" So too, after Dimmesdale's death and Pearl's marriage, Hester can only return to Boston to continue a penance she never understands. Never is she able to reconcile the opposing forces that pull on her. To the end she is the fair Puritan restricted by black Puritanism.

Hester's life of service provides a muted analogue, a solemnizing counterbalance, to Dimmesdale's triumphant gesture of leadership. Most modern critics, following Henry James's reading, have correctly centered on Dimmesdale as the most important character in *The Scarlet Letter*. But Hester's role, while secondary to Dimmesdale's, is necessary for the world view Hawthorne wants to express. Dimmesdale has performed a supreme act. He has seen the world as it is; he has entered it; and he has driven himself toward perfection with wise humility. In all senses of the word he is the Hawthornean *hero*. But he is a representative man only in the Emersonian sense of possessing the highest capabilities of man. Nearer the human norm is Hester. She cannot reconcile the forces of emotion and reasoned restriction to progress as Dimmesdale does. She can merely hold them off from crushing her by leading a life of service to others. We must remember that her somber figure is the last we see in the romance, and that fact greatly influences the romance's tone. Were we to end on Dimmesdale's triumphant gesture the work would not be "a tale of human frailty and sorrow" as Hawthorne called *The Scarlet Letter*, but a paean to human courage and hope. Hawthorne was not that optimistic. Instead he balances Dimmesdale's progress against Hester's lack of progress. The real source of human tragedy in the work is the divergence between the outcomes for the two characters. Hester's dazed, circumscribed, final state of existence is all the more pathetic because of the purpose and direction Dimmesdale found. Starting weaker than Hester, he has far eclipsed her, and so, Hawthorne indicates by closing on Hester, has he eclipsed most other men. At the conclusion of *The Scarlet Letter* we are very much aware that few human beings realize the progress of a Dimmesdale.

This comparison may also be extended to include Chillingworth, for his role also forms an analogue to Dimmesdale's. Like Dimmesdale he has intellectual pride. He refuses to tolerate the imperfection of their sin. Similarly he has a strong emotional drive. It, of course, manifests itself most in his savoring of the hunt. But these elements, which fuse in Dimmesdale for the better, fuse in Chillingworth for the worse. The two men are almost counterparts. The romance ends with a series of alternatives.

Hawthorne's strategy in *The Scarlet Letter*, then, is to enclose his human dilemma between the extreme positions represented by the black Puritan and the fair Puritan and to investigate a range of consequences within those boundaries. The highly structured artifice of the romance keeps the process of the investigation squarely before the reader. We are aware of the artificer setting the characters against each other to explore the possibilities of his conflict of passion and restraint

---

Chapter IV

The House of the Seven Gables: Hawthorne's comedy

After *The Scarlet Letter*, Hawthorne set out deliberately to reverse himself. He had written to Horatio Bridge, "*The Scarlet Letter* is positively a hellfired story, into which I found it almost impossible to throw any cheering light." He intended *The House of
the Seven Gables* to be quite the opposite. It was to be drenched
with "cheering light." After the tragedy of Hester and Dimmesdale, Hawthorne proceeded to write what can only be termed a
comedy. Here it is useful to follow a distinction made by Northrop Frye in *The Anatomy of Criticism*. Whereas tragedy, according to Frye, often narrows a relatively free life into a process

of causation, comedy tends to expand life from subjugation to a harsh or arbitrary law into greater freedom.[1] Dimmesdale and Hester in *The Scarlet Letter* sense more and more the inescapableness of the consequences of their sin, but in *The House of the Seven Gables* the Pyncheons and the Maules move in the opposite direction, toward an eventual release from the sin committed long in the past. We should not consider *The House of the Seven Gables* to be a refutation of *The Scarlet Letter*, however. It is simply another view, and a view inherent in Dimmesdale's redemptive death at the end of *The Scarlet Letter*. In *The House of the Seven Gables* Hawthorne takes what we may call the "long view" of the consequences of sin. He sees evil in the context of a human cycle of evolution and renewal.

The difficulty with this—and let us admit that *The House of the Seven Gables* has its difficulties—is that Hawthorne can convince us of the "truth" of *The Scarlet Letter* much better than he can the "truth" of *The House of the Seven Gables*. He can convince us of the existence of evil and its consequences by chronicling the states of mind that accompany it. But to convince us of a human cycle of renewal he has to ask us to accept, literally believe, the laws of comedy where young lovers always eventually overthrow the prohibitions of tyrannical figures.[2] In *The Scarlet Letter* the world of the romance is measured against life; in *The House of the Seven Gables* it is measured against the conventions and expectations of comedy. There is no reason in the world why the feud of the Pyncheons and the Maules *must* be resolved in the marriage of the last descendants of each line. We have a sense that such is the way the evil *ought* to be resolved, but that is all. In *The Scarlet Letter* we begin with two facts: that Hester and Dimmesdale

1 Frye, *The Anatomy of Criticism* (New York, 1967), p. 212.
2 Frederick Crews has anticipated me in finding *The House of the Seven Gables* to be about the conflict of the authoritarian parental type and weaker characters who resemble children. His interest, however, lies in what this conflict reveals of Hawthorne's Oedipal themes. He forgets Northrop Frye's point that many, if not most, comedies depend on an overthrow of an authoritarian figure. See Crews, "Homely Witchcraft," *The Sins of the Fathers: Hawthorne's Psychological Themes* (New York, 1966), pp. 171–193, and Frye, *Anatomy of Criticism*, p. 164.

are social actors and that they have committed what is taken to be a sin in their community. There is a strong sense of inevitability in the way these two elements converge on Hester and Dimmesdale. Yet we need not know anything about the laws of tragedy to see that this is so. In *The House of the Seven Gables*, however, the argument of renewal does rest squarely on the idea that in Hawthorne's Illyria what *ought* to be will come to pass. All this is to suggest that the concept of artistic distance is very different in *The House of the Seven Gables* than it was in the preceding work.

Hawthorne achieved his distance in *The Scarlet Letter* by going back into the past, by playing with superstitions of the age, and by using ideal patterns to structure his work. These elements are also operative in *The House of the Seven Gables*. Hawthorne works with the action in the present as an extension from the past; he plays more broadly with the supernatural; and he patterns his action in an ideal cycle of renewal. But to this he adds the further distance of comic expectations. The work, then, depends still more on artifice than does *The Scarlet Letter*. Hawthorne seems to have recognized this fact, and he seems to have tried to exploit the idea of the artificiality of his fictional world by flagrant exaggeration.

But before we can investigate Hawthorne's use of artifice, we must have some idea of how Hawthorne presents his "long view" of sin in the human condition. He begins the romance with a comparison between man and nature. He describes the man-made house of the Pyncheons and the elm tree that grows in front of it. The house was erected by Colonel Pyncheon on land he usurped from the Maules. It represents a wrong the Pyncheons have committed, a wrong of the utmost seriousness because Pyncheon was instrumental in having Maule hung for witchcraft in order to stifle Maule's claims to the land. The house, however, exists in the world of nature. The gigantic elm tree covers the whole roof with its foliage. At one point Hawthorne says, "It gave beauty to the old edifice, and seemed to make it a part of nature." [3] Green moss

3 *The House of the Seven Gables*, Centenary Edition (Columbus, 1965), p. 27.

covers the gables. On the roof between two gables are the flower-
shrubs of Alice's posies, which grow in the collected dirt on the
roof. Behind the house is a small, weedy garden and on its sides
plots of grass covered with burdock and leaves. The world of nature gradually renews itself. Thanks to the care of Holgrave and
Phoebe, the garden becomes a pleasant retreat. The tree loses one
branch (symbolic perhaps of the evil represented by Judge Pyncheon), but continues to flourish. A blighted rose bush yields one
perfect rose, and Alice's posies burst into bloom at the romance's
end. Nature is supreme at the conclusion, when the surviving
Pyncheons and Holgrave remove themselves to the country estate
of the Pyncheon family. Like the cycle of nature, the Pyncheons
and the Maules gradually renew themselves over the years. We
see various attempts at renewal at various stages. The shopkeeper
Pyncheon, who tried to break out of the confines of the aristocracy, and the old bachelor who wanted to return the land to the
Maules are examples of such attempts. Also the relationship between Alice Pyncheon and Matthew Maule, a relationship half of
competition of wills and half of attraction, is a step toward the
eventual marriage of Phoebe and Holgrave that terminates the
feud. The two worlds of man and nature come together, at least
in the imagination, when Holgrave in love thinks of the Pyncheon
house as a flowering Eden. Thus, Hawthorne uses the analogy of
nature to point to the theme of human renewal.

The theme as I have outlined it, however, is fairly conventional
material. A brief review of Requier's *The Old Sanctuary* should
make this clear. Comparing *The House of the Seven Gables* with
Requier's work is, of course, complicated by the fact that much
of the subject matter in Hawthorne's romance comes directly
from his family's past, as for instance the feud between the Haw-
thornes and the Englishes that was eventually ended by a marriage.[4] Yet Requier's romance does provide us a chance to see

4 Hawthorne's debts to family tradition have been traced by several
  scholars. The results are nicely summarized in Marcus Cunliffe, "*The
  House of the Seven Gables,*" *Hawthorne Centenary Essays* (Columbus,
  1964), pp. 81–84.

Hawthorne's artistic shaping against a contemporary work with virtually the same kind of material. In *The Old Sanctuary* we found the symbol of the decaying building set against the self-renewing tree precisely as is the case in *The House of the Seven Gables*. The patriarchal ancestor appears in both works, and dies strikingly, flagrantly, in both. The feud of the members of the older generation is solved by the lovers in the younger generation in each work. Quite a lot of the essentials of Hawthorne's work are, then, to be found in the utterly conventional piece of popular fiction.

Where Hawthorne differs most drastically from Requier, as we noted earlier, is in his addition of the comic characters of Clifford and Hepzibah as a sort of middle generation between the vengeful ancestors and the lovestruck young characters. This addition is quite similar to his addition of the complex Dimmesdale between the two poles of the black Puritan and the fair Puritan in *The Scarlet Letter*. But Clifford and Hepzibah are overtly characters of parody. They burlesque the faults of their Pyncheon ancestors and the positive attributes of the young lovers as well. They shift the relatively standard materials of contemporary romance into a new mode.

The Pyncheon ancestor is presented in three guises: Colonel Pyncheon, the originator of the evil in the family line who usurped Maule's land to begin a New World aristocracy; Gervayse Pyncheon, who risked his daughter's well-being for a chance to obtain the deed to land in Maine which could lead to a European title; and Jaffrey Pyncheon, the family representative in the present who induced his uncle's death, shifted the blame to Clifford, plans to force information from Clifford about family wealth, and aspires to the governorship. These men have in common an avaricious pride by which they hope to make themselves immortal, or at least more "real" than other men, by establishing a claim as a head of some kind of dynasty. Hawthorne goes to great lengths to make clear that the claims they seek are unreal and illusory through his use of the missing deed that is granted them by Holgrave only when it is totally worthless. The deed be-

comes known as "an absurd delusion of family importance."
Nonetheless, the Pyncheon ancestor pursues his "deed" at any cost
to the rights of the people around him, with "an iron energy of
purpose."

Coupled with his pride, probably another version of it, is the
Pyncheon ancestor's sensual appetite.[5] This is only hinted at in
Colonel Pyncheon. In his portrait with Bible and sword, he appears to be the archetype of the black Puritan. But on the day of
his house-opening, his home swells with the "Velvet garments,
sombre but rich" of his aristocratic guests. And prepared for the
guests is an enormous feast which Hawthorne records in great detail. A sensual opulence is present in the Colonel's life. Moreover,
a certain sexual appetite is implied in Hawthorne's telling us the
Colonel had "worn out" three wives. Sensual opulence becomes
almost the reason for existence for Gervayse. He converts the
Colonel's parlor into an apartment "provided with furniture, in an
elegant and costly style, principally from Paris; the floor (which
was unusual, at that day) being covered with a carpet, so skilfully
and richly wrought, that it seemed to glow as with living flowers" (p. 193). In the corner is a marble statue of a nude woman,
and by the fireplace a cabinet of ebony inlaid with ivory. Gervayse wears a flowing wig, a coat of blue velvet with lace, and a
gold-flowered waistcoat. He finds American sherry too potent
and prefers the more delicate wines of Italy and France. Signifi-
cantly he gazes at a landscape by Claude, while Maule gains control of his daughter's mind. His act is significant because it was the
lure of the aesthetic world of Europe that brought Pyncheon to
agree to Maule's experiment.[6] This sensual appetite continues in

5 This point is well established and discussed at some length by Darrel
  Abel in "Hawthorne's House of Tradition," *South Atlantic Quarterly,*
  LII (October, 1953), 561–578. Abel maintains that Gervayse's life is a
  progression from the Colonel's covetousness and luxury, and that Clifford's Sybaritism is a decaying progression from them both. I wish to present his argument from a slightly different vantage point, that of seeing
  parody put against straightforward presentation of a theme.
6 Cf. Leo B. Levy, "Picturesque Style in *The House of the Seven Gables,*"
  New England Quarterly, XXXIX (June, 1966), 154. Levy offers a fuller

the Judge, and it becomes at times almost crude. We learn, for instance, that Jaffrey has had attacks of gout and has "limited" himself to five diurnal glasses of old sherry. One of the worst taunts
Hawthorne throws at the Judge's corpse is the news that Jaffrey
will miss a rich dinner with his political friends. As with the Colonel's, Hawthorne describes the dinner in detail, but here he specifically emphasizes the Judge's craving in a way he had not with
the Colonel. He refers to Jaffrey's "ogre-like appetite." With pol-
ished boots, gold-headed cane, and white linen neck-cloth, the
Judge seems the very model of decorum. Yet when he tries to be-
stow a kiss on Phoebe, she finds him a little more sensual than the
occasion requires. And we learn at the end that Jaffrey was profli-
gate in youth just as is his son. The twin strains of pride and sen-
suousness, then, run in the Pyncheon family. The first is parodied
in Hepzibah, and the second in Clifford.

Hepzibah's experience of opening the store makes a mockery of
the Pyncheon concept of pride. Hawthorne refers to the episode
as "the final throe of what called itself old gentility." Hepzibah
seems to continue the frown discovered on the Colonel's face
when his guests found his corpse, but Hepzibah's look does not
result from aristocratic severity, only from nearsightedness. Her
fear of the door creaking open to admit her first cash customer,
Ned Higgins, the cannibal of Jim Crows, mocks the suspense of
the preceding chapter when the door swung open onto the view
of the dead Colonel. Hawthorne's language changes noticeably in
the chapters on Hepzibah from what it was previously. He is
much more present as a commentator, and he packs his sentences
with polysyllabic words and near clichés, creating a mock-heroic
effect: "Our story must therefore await Miss Hepzibah at the
threshold of her chamber; only presuming, meanwhile, to note
some of the heavy sighs that labored from her bosom, with little
restraint as to their lugubrious depth and volume of sound, inas-
much as they could be audible to nobody, save a disembodied lis-
tener like ourself" (p. 30). Furthermore, he views Hepzibah, from

---

analysis of the function of this painting toward the theme of the romance.

a distance, in absurd positions: "As her rigid and rusty frame goes down upon its hands and knees, in quest of the absconding marbles..." (p. 37). But the real source of the humor in the episode is Hepzibah's fear of confronting her customers. Hawthorne describes her as one "who had fed herself from childhood with the shadowy food of aristocratic reminiscences, and whose religion it was, that a lady's hand soils itself irremediably by doing aught for bread" (p. 37). She can listen to Holgrave's advice that the concepts of gentleman and lady "imply, not privilege, but restriction," and she can grow angry at a lady she sees in the street for whom the world must toil "that the palms of her hands may be kept white and delicate," and yet whenever the time comes that Hepzibah must treat with her customers, her pride makes the encounter a "dreaded crisis." She is the victim of her pride and of the general ineptness that has resulted from a lifetime of prideful isolation. To be sure, Hawthorne shows much of the episode from Hepzibah's point of view, and this wins a good deal of our sympathy for her. Yet this makes her no less a mockery of the pride of the Pyncheon ancestor. Lest we miss Hawthorne's point, he compares his turbaned heroine later to the crested hens who stalk peevishly through the weedy garden of the Pyncheon house. Both Hepzibah and the hens are mockeries of the Pyncheons who would lead dynasties.

Clifford is a more complicated character. Like Hepzibah, he is an epitome of the isolation and decay of the Pyncheons, but in his attempts to break free of his isolation he brings us as close as we come to a pivotal consciousness in the work. In this study, however, we are considering him mainly as a character of parody. Clifford cuts a ludicrous figure. He affects the elegant dress of the Pyncheons, but his dressing gown of damask, faded after thirty years, is a poor substitute for the stylish dress of Gervayse and Jaffrey. He has the Pyncheon appetite. This is made clear to us when we see him first at the breakfast table. Hawthorne describes his expression: "It was a look of appetite. He ate food with what might almost be termed voracity, and seemed to forget himself, Hepzibah, the young girl, and everything else around him, in the

sensual enjoyment which the bountifully spread table afforded"
(p. 107). When he finishes, he cries like a pampered child for
more. Most of all, in a half-torpid state Clifford savors the beautiful and abhors the ugly. He is governed entirely by his sense of
the beautiful. He delights in Phoebe's presence, but has to turn his
eyes away from Hepzibah. He enjoys the music of the street or-
gan, but cries when he sees the ugly monkey of the organ-grinder.
Because of his incapacity to bear any of the world's harshness, he
virtually cuts himself off from the mainstream of life. This is demonstrated by his act of blowing delicate and beautiful soap bubbles
from his arched window to passersby. This is the nearest Clifford
can come to an act of communication. Certainly Colonel Pyncheon and Gervayse would disown his torpor and effeminacy, and
Jaffrey is icily contemptuous of his ludicrousness in blowing bubbles from the window. But all share, in varying degrees, Clifford's
sensuous desire for the world of beauty of an aristocracy. He is a
lunatic version of their obsession.

Together, Clifford and Hepzibah form a pair of mock lovers.
The progression of their reunion parallels the development of the
love of Holgrave and Phoebe. To understand how this is so we
must look first at the relatively conventional pair of romantic lovers. The love of Holgrave and Phoebe develops in three stages.

In the first stage their differences are defined. Holgrave is a radical reformer. He is a member of what R. W. B. Lewis in *The
American Adam* calls "Young America" or the "party of hope."
Holgrave would free the American from any dependency on tradition and the accomplishments of his ancestors and make him
solely dependent on the present and his own merits. On these
grounds he attacks the House of the Seven Gables in particular
and houses from the past in general. His attack must strike us as
somewhat ironic since we have to assume he himself is caught up
in the past wrong done his family by the Pyncheons. Curiosity
about the past, if not the desire for revenge, must have brought
him to the house. Hawthorne is explicit in his judgment of Holgrave as a reformer. He finds him too radical and too egotistical:
"His error lay, in supposing that this age, more than any past or

future one, is destined to see the tattered garments of Antiquity exchanged for a new suit, instead of gradually renewing themselves by patchwork; in applying his own little life-span as the measure of an interminable achievement; and, more than all, in fancying that it mattered anything to the great end in view, whether he himself should contend for it or against it" (p. 180). But Hawthorne quickly adds that Holgrave's "faith in man's brightening destiny" is one of mankind's most important props. Without it there is little reason for man to live. Hawthorne admires Holgrave's positiveness but mocks his stiff-necked radicalism. Phoebe, with a conservatism biologically common to Hawthorne's women, also distrusts Holgrave's radicalism. "He may set the house on fire" is her first reaction when Hepzibah tells her about Holgrave. Phoebe is modern to the extent of being a good shopkeeper, but she has also a conservative strain that leads her to fear things outside the ordinary. Again Hawthorne is explicit: "The girl's was not one of those natures which are most attracted by what is strange and exceptional in human character. The path, which would best have suited her, was the well-worn track of ordinary life" (p. 142).

Their relationship moves into its second stage after Holgrave has read his story of Alice Pyncheon to Phoebe.[7] Holgrave's gestures put Phoebe completely in his control in a state of semi-hypnosis. He refuses to take advantage of his control, however, and he gradually comes to realize that love for Phoebe is the source of his refusal. Holgrave speaks of a "second youth, gushing out of the heart's joy at being in love." "Could I keep the feeling that now possesses me," he tells Phoebe, "... the house ... would be

7 Here I draw on the work of two critics who have looked at the development of the love relationship: Maurice Beebe, "The Fall of the House of Pyncheon," *Nineteenth-Century Fiction,* XI (June, 1956), 1–17, and Francis Battaglia, "*The House of the Seven Gables:* New Light on Old Problems," *PMLA,* LXXXII (December, 1967), 579–590. Battaglia's article is particularly helpful. He traces the developments in the relationship in order to show that the marriage at the end is adequately prepared for in advance. What he fails to notice is that the development would be simple to the extent of sentimentalism or banality if it were not for the counterbalancing parody by Clifford and Hepzibah.

like a bower in Eden" (p. 214). And interestingly enough, he begins to mock his radicalism and think of reform through love:
"Moonlight, and the sentiment in man's heart, responsive to it, is
the greatest of renovators and reformers. And all other reform
and renovation, I suppose, will prove to be no better than moon-
shine!" (p. 214).[8] Only later, when Clifford notices a change in
her, does Phoebe realize that she too is in love. But during the
conversation with Holgrave, she admits to him that the moonlight
has presented the world in a charming way which she, as a practical young woman accustomed only to the plain ordinariness of
broad daylight, has never witnessed before. All that is lacking at
this point in their relationship is a mutual realization and declaration of their love.

At this juncture Hawthorne suspends their development as
Phoebe goes to the country, and shifts the action to the death of
the Judge and to the flight of Hepzibah and Clifford. When he
resumes their development at the third stage, he has removed the
last obstacle to their love. Jaffrey's death wipes out the last of the
dangerously avaricious Pyncheons, and Holgrave can reasonably
consider himself free from the family feud. In the excitement of
finding Phoebe immediately after the discovery of Jaffrey's death,
Holgrave experiences a feeling of release and tells Phoebe he loves
her. At this moment he is as free from the tyranny of the past as
he probably will ever be, and in this situation he changes his radical position against institutions of the past. He argues now, sym-
bolically, for a house of stone which can be altered on the inside
by each generation. In other words, he argues now for a compromise between traditions of the past and changes in the present. He
has come away from his unbending radical position to the more
moderate version Hawthorne alluded to in his metaphor of the

8 The declarations of young men in the first burst of love are always a
little suspect. Surely we cannot believe Holgrave has instantly thrown
over his ideas of political and institutional reform. We can accept, however, that he seems to have mellowed somewhat in his views and at least
seems to have some fuller concern for attitudes of individuals as well as
for external forms of living. This change, as Francis Battaglia has shown,
helps us accept his greater change at the romance's end.

patched garment in his criticism of Holgrave. Phoebe too changes. She moves away from being the timid creature frightened by Holgrave's challenging attitudes. When he tells her he will be a contented man rather than a reformer, she replies, "I would not have it so!" And Hawthorne tells us she spoke "earnestly." Whether or not she has the power to control his domestication completely is immaterial. The fact is she has broadened her perspective to the extent where she can appreciate his urge to see mankind improve. Holgrave, on his side, has gained a relaxed tolerance for institutions of the past. Specifically in his case, he gains an estate and wealth with which to begin and continue a family. He accepts a place in tradition.

The Pyncheons and the Maules will be regenerated by the marriage of the young lovers, and Holgrave and Phoebe grow in stature through their relationship. These results, if left by themselves, would be utterly banal. They are the stuff of *The Old Sanctuary.* They would make up a comedy in which the forces of evil were overthrown so easily and so quickly that the work would be without substance—a *Winter's Tale* without the hardship undergone by Leontes. Fortunately Hawthorne does not let this development stand by itself; he parallels it with the relationship of Clifford and Hepzibah and gives us a counterbalancing parody of his young lovers.

When Hepzibah brings out and dreams over her miniature portrait of Clifford, she prompts Hawthorne to muse: "Can it have been an early lover of Miss Hepzibah?" (p. 32). After Clifford's return, Hawthorne writes of her: "How patiently did she endeavor to wrap Clifford up in her great, warm love, and make it all the world to him, so that he should retain no torturing sense of the coldness and dreariness, without!" (p. 134). Hepzibah is "in love" with her brother. This is not to say, however, as Frederick Crews has tried to show, that Hawthorne is treating the idea of incest. Hepzibah is too much the comic type of the old maid for us to consider her seriously in such a role. This is to say simply that the only love Hepzibah is capable of pursuing is the safely platonic one of sister for brother. This is as near to romantic love as she can come. Her love allows her all of the sentiment of romantic love with none of the danger of its passion. In much the same way, Clifford can follow his interest in women only at a great distance from them. His distant interest in Phoebe exemplifies this: "On Clifford's part, it was the feeling of a man naturally endowed with the liveliest sensibility to feminine influence, but who had never quaffed the cup of passionate love, and knew that it was now too late. . . . Thus, his sentiment for Phoebe, without being paternal, was not less chaste than if she had been his daughter. He was a man, it is true, and recognized her as a woman. She was his only representative of womankind" (p. 141). Hepzibah's pursuit of Clifford, then, is the pursuit of one attenuated lover for another.

The initial block to their love is Hepzibah's ugliness. Because of his overdeveloped sensitivity, Clifford can scarcely bear to look at his devoted sister or listen to her croaking voice. She can be near him, for the most part, only when he dozes in his chair. Selflessly, Hepzibah sends Phoebe to him in his waking hours to please him. This is true until Jaffrey's death. Then Clifford, excited by a feeling of release similar to Holgrave's, offers to take Hepzibah away, presumably to begin a new life with him, Hepzibah's fondest wish. He is hardly romantic, however. "Put on your cloak and hood," he tells her, "or whatever it pleases you to wear! No matter what; —you cannot look beautiful nor brilliant, my poor Hepzibah! Take your purse, with money in it, and come along!" (p. 251). They set out "like children." But they are children "in their inexperience," not in Holgrave's projected state of second innocence.

On the train, Clifford, so long afraid of new elements in his love, speaks of the promise of the future as the radical Holgrave has done. He talks of human progress as an "ascending spiral curve," wants to abolish homes in favor of a nomadic existence, and puts forward a crackpot theory of electricity as "the all-pervading intelligence" by which lovers may "send their heart-throbs from Maine to Florida." Hepzibah, like Phoebe, fears the idea of leaving behind the ways of life with which she is familiar. While Clifford speaks of abolishing houses, she sees the House of the

Seven Gables wherever she looks. When the pair leaves the train, Clifford feels his energy subsiding and reluctantly puts himself in Hepzibah's charge: "You must take the lead now, Hepzibah! . . . Do with me as you will!" (p. 266). He surrenders himself to Hepzibah in an exaggerated anticipation of Holgrave's surrender of his radicalism before Phoebe.

The rapprochement of Clifford and Hepzibah is almost a farcical representation of the love of Holgrave and Phoebe. The older couple are signally less successful than their younger counterparts. Clifford settles for Hepzibah's care because he cannot sustain the strength to push out further into life. We are told he retains some of his new energy, enough at least to make him happy in his idyllic life at the Pyncheon country seat, but we can hardly consider him to be more than at peace with Hepzibah in their seclusion with Holgrave and Phoebe. The younger couple, on the other hand, we may assume, do enter into life in the sense of beginning a marriage and a family. We get, then, a balance of the two couples. The balance is particularly noticeable because the flight of Hepzibah and Clifford is placed between the realization of love by the young characters and their declaration of the love. Hawthorne invites comparison of the two sets of couples. The modified success of Clifford and Hepzibah points up the artificiality of the complete and easy success of Holgrave and Phoebe.[9]

The structure of *The House of the Seven Gables*, as we have now seen, depends on a rhythm of straightforward presentation counterpointed with comic inversion. The prideful building of the house is followed by the episode of Hepzibah's fear of serving customers. The section on Clifford's Sybaritism precedes the story of Gervayse's longings for the aesthetic life of Europe. And the

9 Cf. William B. Dillingham, "Structure and Theme in *The House of the Seven Gables*," *Nineteenth-Century Fiction*, XIV (June, 1959), 59–70. Dillingham holds that the ending is ironic. Perfect happiness is not achieved because Hepzibah and Clifford have shown they cannot break free of their isolation. The problem with his argument is that he slights the progress made by Holgrave and Phoebe. The two sets of lovers must be weighed against each other. When we do this, we find the happiness at the end considerably "modified," but we do not find it overthrown.

flight of Clifford and Hepzibah comes in the midst of the developing love of Holgrave and Phoebe.

Hawthorne even balances a serious metaphorical statement of
his theme against a comic inversion. The metaphor is his typical
metaphor for life, the festive procession. The straightforward
presentation of it involves a political parade "with hundreds of
flaunting banners, and drums, fifes, clarions, and cymbals, rever-
berating between the rows of buildings" (p. 165). Hawthorne
states that if the spectator sees it close up, individual by individual,
he will find it "fool's play." But if he gains a wider or fuller perspective of its whole, he will sense an enormous human energy in
the procession.

> In order to become majestic, it should be viewed from some vantage-
> point, as it rolls its slow and long array through the centre of a wide
> plain, or the stateliest public square of a city; for then, by its re-
> moteness, it melts all the petty personalities, of which it is made up,
> into one broad mass of existence—one great life—one collected body
> of mankind, with a vast, homogeneous spirit animating it. But, on
> the other hand, if an impressible person, standing alone over the
> brink of one of these processions, should behold it, not in its atoms,
> but in its aggregate—as a mighty river of life, massive in its tide, and
> black with mystery, and, out of its depths, calling to the kindred
> depth within him—then the contiguity would add to the effect. It
> might so fascinate him that he would hardly be restrained from
> plunging into the surging stream of human sympathies [p. 165].

The passage is Hawthorne's endorsement of the "long view" of
life with the great potential residing in its energy. It is easily his
most eloquent summary of the romance's theme. Yet it is preceded by a counterbalancing arrangement of figures in the show-
case of the organ-grinder.

> In all their variety of occupation—the cobbler, the blacksmith, the
> soldier, the lady with her fan, the toper with his bottle, the milk-
> maid sitting by her cow—this fortunate little society might truly be
> said to enjoy a harmonious existence, and to make life literally a
> dance. The Italian turned a crank; and, behold! every one of these
> small individuals started into the most curious vivacity. The cobbler
> wrought upon a shoe; the blacksmith hammered his iron; the soldier
> waved his glittering blade; . . . all at the same turning of a crank.

Yes; and, moved by the self-same impulse, a lover saluted his mistress on her lips! Possibly, some cynic, at once merry and bitter, had desired to signify, in this pantomimic scene, that we mortals, whatever our business or amusement—however serious, however trifling—all dance to one identical tune, and, in spite of our ridiculous activity, bring nothing finally to pass [p. 163].

This show directly mocks the other. Whereas energy is the main attribute of the one, stasis is the chief characteristic of the other. The one is rich and mysterious; the other mechanical. The one exhibits the potential for harmonious development; the other shows "nothing finally [comes] to pass." To be sure, Hawthorne rejects the "cynical" moral of the organ-grinder's show, but he rejects it only after he has pictured it at some length. The two views—Hawthorne's and the cynic's—demonstrate the possibility of looking at the procession of life from several perspectives. Hawthorne has elected the more optimistic one and rejected the other out of hand. The fact that he gives the alternative perspective and parodies his view with a dumb show illustrates a certain arbitrariness in the work. Hawthorne has chosen to present one view, but *sotto voce* he admits there are others. This emphasizes the process of searching for meaning in the work. In the confines of the romance, we are asked to see life mainly within the comic mode, but we are made aware of other possibilities too, as Hawthorne conducts a dialectic between two voices, the voice of the *alazon* and the voice of the *eiron*.

Hawthorne emphasizes artifice in at least two other ways that are related to each other. Both involve his techniques of narration. The first is the relatively simple device of the story-within-the-story told by Holgrave. Here Hawthorne raises one of his characters just about to his own level as artificer. The story Holgrave tells has obvious thematic importance. As we have already noted, it shows us the sensual appetite of the Pyncheon ancestor. Also it presents us with a Maule in the act of controlling a Pyncheon through mesmerism. The act reveals the Maules to be almost as guilty of enforcing their will on others as the Pyncheons are. In their quest for revenge, the Maules go about as far beyond the

limits of sympathetic ties between human beings as the Pyncheons
went in usurping the land. Matthew Maule's destruction of Alice
Pyncheon forms a contrast with Holgrave's act of sympathy and
love in the present when he refuses to control Phoebe. We can
measure Holgrave's progress away from the ruthlessness of his
ancestors. But what is just as important, we find the levels of
reality in the book are becoming blurred.[10] Storytelling has become an integral part of the action.

The other way Hawthorne emphasizes artifice is by reducing
himself just about to the level of his characters. This he does in
his chapter "Governor Pyncheon" where Hawthorne taunts the
dead body of Jaffrey. This scene also has great bearing on the romance's central meaning. Hawthorne very firmly links here in
the Judge the sensual appetite of the Pyncheons (best shown by
Gervayse) and their prideful desire for an aristocratic position
(best shown by the Colonel) through the description of the political dinner where food and political power are being devoured
simultaneously. Hawthorne also shows a merging of the Judge's
watch time into a cyclical time of renewal. For Jaffrey time is a
mere means of stringing together appointments largely for his
self-gain. His day consists of appointments with Clifford, at the
insurance office, at the bank, with a broker, at an auction, with a
horse-seller, with a political committee to give a donation, perhaps with a widow who needs financial aid, with his physician,
and at the dinner where he expects to be named candidate for gov-

10 The levels of reality at one point become too confused. In Holgrave's
   story, Matthew Maule apparently does not know where the Pyncheon
   deed is hidden. He hypnotizes Alice in order to find out if she can
   locate it through a kind of extrasensory perception. If we assume Maule
   knew where the deed was all along, he would be more sinister than
   Holgrave generally represents him as being. But in Hawthorne's story,
   Holgrave knows precisely where the deed is hidden and how to get at it.
   The question we must ask is how could Holgrave know where the deed
   was if Matthew did not know. The chances of the secret being passed
   down to Holgrave without passing through the possession of Matthew
   are slight. If Holgrave is deliberately misrepresenting Matthew Maule,
   Hawthorne should eventually let us know this more definitely. But what
   is probably the case is that Hawthorne missed this detail of plot in the
   confusion of his levels of reality.

ernor. As his watch runs down and stops, another kind of time takes over: "Ah! The watch has at last ceased to tick. . . . But the great world-clock of Time still keeps its beat" (pp. 281–282). The small meanness of the Judge's life is absorbed into a greater natural cycle of renewal, Hawthorne tells us as he develops the scene. The evil the Judge represents will be left behind as the day leaves behind the night. More interesting than the thematic relevance of the scene, however, is the way it is presented. Virtually every critic to write on *The House of the Seven Gables* has remarked on the fact that Hawthorne himself enters the work to tonguelash his villain with scornful irony.[11] At one point, for instance, Hawthorne rails at the Judge with the rhetoric of a Puritan minister in the white heat of a damnation sermon: "Rise up, thou subtile, worldly, selfish, iron-hearted hypocrite, and make thy choice, whether still to be subtile, worldly, selfish, iron-hearted, and hypocritical, or to tear these sins out of thy nature, though they bring the life-blood with them! The Avenger is upon thee! Rise up, before it be too late!" (p. 283). With direct addresses like this one, Hawthorne behaves as if he were a character talking to his equal in Jaffrey. He is flouting the artifice of his work. He enters it in a way similar to the way the modern writer André Gide enters his novel *The Counterfeiters* to comment on the characters he has invented. We should note that Hawthorne enters *The House of the*

11 Two of the most interesting critics are Austin Warren, "Nathaniel Hawthorne," *Rage for Order* (Chicago, 1948), p. 102, and Crews, *The Sins of the Fathers*, pp. 175–177. Warren feels the characterization of Jaffrey is out of balance with the others. He says, "everyone is successively seen from inside, seen with some sympathy, except Pyncheon." Probably Warren is too concerned with the need for "round" characters of realistic fiction. The villain, or "blocking figure," is absolutely necessary for Hawthorne's comedy, and too much sympathy for him would destroy the comedy. Crews feels the vehemence with which Hawthorne assaults the Judge can only be explained if we see Hawthorne attacking the archetypal father figure. (Hawthorne's father disappeared at sea when Hawthorne was very young.) Crews may well be right, but his analysis of the author's unconscious motivation is way outside the scope of this study. Still, his idea is worth some consideration here if only because it raises questions about the relationship of conscious artistic creating and unconscious motivation.

Seven Gables fairly often. The scene where he presents himself in Hepzibah's chamber while she is rising is an example of this. But nowhere else does he maintain his presence in the action as long as in the Judge's death scene. In this scene he unmistakably calls attention to his presence.

So Hawthorne raises a character to the level of storyteller and reduces himself to the level of character at two instances in *The House of the Seven Gables*. In both instances we are made more aware of the figure of the artificer and the intermingling of artifice with the supposedly real world of the fiction.

What does Hawthorne try to gain by this emphasis on the artfulness of *The House of the Seven Gables*? Most obviously, he gains artistic distance from the reader and cuts down the empathy the reader may wish to feel for the characters. But this is really no more than restating the question. What does Hawthorne try to gain by distance? Certainly not the clarity of vision which he sought in *The Scarlet Letter*. Distance here depends on statement and mockery of statement, and this technique complicates more than it clarifies. Above all what Hawthorne makes us aware of is that this is *just a story*, one way of looking at life. He assures us that there are other ways. This way is merely the most optimistic. It is the comic view where all ends well. *The House of the Seven Gables* gives us life at its conceivable best. Hawthorne implies he would be well satisfied if we take it as a possibility, not a verity, against which to measure our lives. He has moved beyond verities. And that is precisely the sense he communicates through his emphasis on artifice.

Chapter v

The Blithedale Romance:
Hawthorne's dark, ironic drama
of masters and slaves

In *The Blithedale Romance* Hawthorne's tragic sense and comic sense come together in irony.[1] The major events of the work, if we were to take them head on, would be unquestionably tragic.

1 The one critic who also sees the work as a clash of comic and tragic visions is Roy Male, "The Pastoral Wasteland: *The Blithedale Romance*," *Hawthorne's Tragic Vision* (Austin, Tex., 1957), pp. 139–156. He remarks, "The failure of Blithedale may be summed up as a misplaced faith in the comic vision of life as a mode of emotional conversion." He wishes to argue for the establishment of a tragic vision. I feel the texture of the work is better seen by concentrating on the clash of the modes than by arguing for the primacy of one.

They concern various kinds of betrayal of human ties. But they
do not come to us head on. They come obliquely, through our
narrator, the comic, fumbling Miles Coverdale.[2] Only when we
encounter the grimly realistic description of Zenobia's corpse,
rigid, jabbed by the grappling hook, do we fully understand the
essential seriousness of the events that have been told us off-
handedly by Coverdale. This scene dominates the romance. Although Hawthorne hurries us to the ironic ending of Coverdale's
blushing, foot-scraping confession of love, the effect of the death

2 Most of the recent criticism of *The Blithedale Romance* centers in the
question of the role of the narrator, and the romance has been well
served by this criticism. William Van O'Connor, "Conscious Naivete in
The Blithedale Romance," *Revue des langues vivantes*, XX (1954), 37–
45, argues that Coverdale's failings as a narrator shape the book. Frederick C. Crews, "A New Reading of *The Blithedale Romance*," *American Literature*, XXIX (May, 1957), 147–170, extends this idea to the
point of finding it to be one of the book's major themes. Coverdale
wishes to shape imaginatively the lives of real people and confuses
aesthetic longings with moral consciousness. In return, William Hedges,
"Hawthorne's *Blithedale*: The Function of the Narrator," *Nineteenth-
Century Fiction*, XIV (March, 1960), 303–316, tries to rescue Coverdale
from some of Crews's charges. He maintains that Coverdale's narration
can be trusted more than Crews will admit, and Hedges even goes so far
as to claim Coverdale learns from the story he tells, as evidenced by his
confession at the end. Crews, then, enlarges his argument in "Turning
the Affair into a Ballad," *The Sins of the Fathers: Hawthorne's Psychological Themes* (New York, 1966), pp. 194–212. Not only does Coverdale
wish to turn the affair into a ballad, Mr. Crews says, but he wishes to
turn it into a series of Oedipal situations. Finally, Kelley Griffith, Jr.,
"Form in *The Blithedale Romance*," *American Literature*, XL (March,
1968), 15–26, and Nina Baym, "*The Blithedale Romance*: A Radical
Reading," *JEGP*, LXVIII (October, 1968), 545–569, discuss the narrator
as the main element of form. "The form of *Blithedale* ...," Griffith says,
"is like that of an interior monologue, which represents the narrator's
illogical thought processes and his attempts to shift events in his mind."
Similarly, Baym views the action as a projection of Coverdale's desires,
in his private quest to find the "soul's reservoir of energy." Obviously,
as the reader will see, I am indebted to this series of debates about
Coverdale. Rather than enter it directly and reiterate what has been said
before, I have tried to concentrate on the way Coverdale's actions differ
from those of the characters he describes and on the effect of the ironic
separation of the narrator from his subjects. In other words, I assume the
tradition of separation established by the critics above.

scene succeeds in coloring the rest of the book. The one look at grim reality is enough to make us aware that real people capable of real suffering exist just beyond the comprehension of the witless narrator. By fitting together, on our own, Coverdale's observations and speculations, we can deduce the dark motives of the other characters. *The Blithedale Romance*, then, is a further experiment in artifice for Hawthorne. He presents a series of tragic events through a comic narrator, and the result is an ironic clash. What is gained by this clash is exactly what we should now be prepared to expect in Hawthorne's romances—action put at a distance so that the process of the writer's organizing meaning in the work becomes prominent.

The ironic clash of views, of course, is not Hawthorne's only means to artistic distance. As we noted earlier, he also relies on the relatively mysterious setting of the experimental community to separate the events of the book from those of the everyday world. It is usual to think of *Blithedale* as the most realistic of Hawthorne's works since so much of it comes directly from Hawthorne's journals, as he himself is quick to point out in his Preface. Yet the impact of the opening chapters is quite the opposite. Hawthorne establishes the everyday world of Boston only, it seems, to break away from it. When Coverdale and his companions leave town, the snowstorm obliterates their tracks and separates them from what they left behind. They are welcomed to Blithedale by Zenobia, who, with her exotic flower in her hair, her beauty, and her forcefulness, seems to Coverdale a kind of enchantress. Then Coverdale, looking out on the farm at night in the snow, sees it as "a lifeless copy of the world in marble." All these elements emphasize the strangeness of the new world Coverdale has moved into.

Set at the distance of romance theory, a highly structured series of parallel relationships asserts itself. The relationships have to do with one character's power over another. Hawthorne directs our attention to this kind of a relationship with the conscious artifice of a story-within-a-story. Zenobia's narrative about the Veiled Lady and the circumstances in which it is told give us a neat vignette of the larger action in *The Blithedale Romance*.[3] The story concerns a young man named Theodore who wants to discover the identity of the clairvoyant known as the Veiled Lady. She presents him with three choices. The first is for him to abandon his search. But since this is out of the question for him, she tells him he may either kiss her through her veil and then lift it, or he may lift the veil without kissing her, in "scornful scepticism and idle curiosity." In the one, he would discover her identity, having made a commitment to her, and in the other, without commitment. If he chooses the kiss, the commitment, the lady will be his for the rest of his life, and if not, he will lose her. Theodore, we remember, takes the latter choice only to discover a lovely face that vanishes from his life forever.

Most obviously this story-within-a-story summarizes the probings of Miles Coverdale. He pries into the lives of Hollingsworth, Zenobia, and Priscilla, without ever making a commitment to them, and one by one he loses them. On the most literal level, Coverdale, like Theodore, discovers the identity of the Veiled Lady in Priscilla and then allows her to vanish from his life, despite his confession that he loved her, because of his inability to make a commitment to her.

At the same time that the story exposes Coverdale's shortcomings, it also gives away Zenobia. She offers the story as the evening's entertainment, but her real motive is to torture Priscilla. Zenobia makes up the story shortly after the visit of Westervelt to Blithedale. We may reasonably assume that Westervelt has told Zenobia of Priscilla's past and has warned Zenobia of the threat to her inheritance, in order to enlist Zenobia's aid to return Priscilla to him. Zenobia, with this knowledge, has Priscilla stand before

3 Cf. Frank Davidson, "Toward a Re-evaluation of *The Blithedale Romance*," *New England Quarterly*, XXV (September, 1952), 374–383. Davidson finds the "veil" to be the work's central symbol. He states that all the characters mask secrets and that the romance is about the difficulty of seeing beneath the masks. I agree. But I think equally important to Hawthorne are the motives of the man who seeks to look beneath the veil and his willingness to assume the ties of responsibility that knowing another person entails.

her while she works out her fictionalized version of Priscilla's past. The story is a torture to Priscilla, because she wants to escape all connection with her past on the stage. Yet the important thing to note here is not just that Zenobia tortures Priscilla, but also that she does it almost wantonly. In rational terms, there is nothing for Zenobia to "gain" by the torture. If she wanted to rid herself of a threat to her inheritance and to her relationship with Hollingsworth, she would have been better off by quietly sending Priscilla to Boston with Westervelt. No, the act is an almost gratuitous act of human cruelty. It resembles the willful act of a master exerting his power over an emotional slave for the sheer joy of it.

The master-slave relationship is apparent from the first meeting of the two sisters. Priscilla, whose father told her fairy-tale stories of Zenobia, drops to her knees and gazes at Zenobia, looking for some sign of sympathy. Even Coverdale must remark: "There occurred to me no mode of accounting for Priscilla's behavior, except by supposing that she had read some of Zenobia's stories . . . and had come hither with the one purpose of being her slave." [4] Zenobia reacts with sharp disdain, until Hollingsworth rebukes her. Later she tells Coverdale, "There is no pleasure in tormenting a person of one's own sex, even if she do favor one with a little more love than one can conveniently dispose of" (p. 34). But this does not prove true. The surfeit of love that Priscilla has for Zenobia makes Priscilla vulnerable to Zenobia. Zenobia cannot resist taking advantage of the vulnerability.

Two scenes should make this clear. The first is the scene where Zenobia caresses Priscilla and leads her to believe she has found the loving sister she wants. "She went towards Priscilla, took her hand, and passed her own rosy finger-tips, with a pretty, caressing movement, over the girl's hair. The touch had a magical effect. So vivid a look of joy flushed up beneath those fingers, that it seemed as if the sad and wan Priscilla had been snatched away, and another kind of creature substituted in her place. This one caress, bestowed voluntarily by Zenobia, was evidently received as a pledge of all

4 *The Blithedale Romance and Fanshawe,* Centenary Edition (Columbus, 1964), p. 33.

that the stranger sought from her, whatever the unuttered boon might be" (pp. 34–35). The caress, a gesture of sympathy and love in itself, ultimately proves cruel, for it serves to draw Priscilla to Zenobia only to increase her vulnerability. The second scene demonstrates this cruelty. It consists of Zenobia decking out Priscilla with flowers, an act apparently like the caress. But here Zenobia covertly mocks Priscilla by ruining the total effect with a weed.

> Zenobia—who showed no conscience in such matters—had also rifled a cherry-tree of one of its blossomed boughs; and, with all this variety of sylvan ornament, had been decking out Priscilla. Being done with a good deal of taste, it made her look more charming than I should have thought possible, with my recollection of the wan, frost-nipt girl, as heretofore described. Nevertheless, among those fragrant blossoms, and conspicuously, too, had been stuck a weed of evil odor and ugly aspect, which, as soon as I detected it, destroyed the effect of all the rest [pp. 58–59].

As with the story-within-a-story, Zenobia's act serves no purpose except to satisfy a sadistic impulse. She has not learned that Priscilla is her sister at this point. But she does sense that Priscilla is a younger rival for Hollingsworth, and she does sense that she has Priscilla in her power emotionally. So she exerts her power.

If we put the two scenes together, we have Zenobia leading Priscilla on more deeply into an emotional bondage so that Zenobia can exercise her power over her. This, perhaps, is to suggest too much scheming behind Zenobia's action. Such, I think, is not the case. In one instance she chooses to accept Priscilla's love, and in another she chooses to use it to mock the girl. She vacillates. Yet the effect is much the same as if Zenobia had schemed. She ends by playing a game of attraction and repulsion with Priscilla when the more honest course, certainly, would be to declare herself a rival to Priscilla.

The gesture of ruining the decorations on Priscilla, so trivial in itself, is indicative of Zenobia's later acts of cruelty. As the stakes increase and Priscilla becomes a greater threat to Zenobia, Zenobia's cruelty increases. Gratuitous cruelty commingles with rational cruelty. Her story of the Veiled Lady is one example of this which we have already seen. Worse is her act of turning Priscilla over to Westervelt. This is the greatest betrayal Zenobia could pay her sister, since Priscilla originally had come to her pleading for protection from her past life. Zenobia betrays everything Priscilla had hoped to find in her. The aim here for Zenobia seems more rational than irrational. Zenobia has, we may assume from the evidence, persuaded Hollingsworth to help her send Priscilla back to Westervelt, in order to protect Zenobia's inheritance which Hollingsworth can then gain through marriage. Yet Zenobia is aware of the cruelty of her betrayal to her sister. In front of Coverdale Zenobia gives away her remorse. Coverdale says: "I could not understand the look of melancholy kindness with which Zenobia regarded her. She advanced a step, and beckoning Priscilla near her, kissed her cheek; then, with a slight gesture of repulse, she moved to the other side of the room" (p. 169). Zenobia makes a gesture of love, as she did in the caress scene. Then, upset by the thought of her betrayal of Priscilla, Zenobia repulses Priscilla and begins a sarcastic baiting of Coverdale. This demonstrates the genuine ambivalence in Zenobia's attitude toward Priscilla. Zenobia recognizes Priscilla's love and trust, partly wants to accept it, but proceeds with her plan, revolted by the way she is betraying Priscilla's love and trust. Whatever feeling she has for Priscilla is far outweighed by her desire to hold Hollingsworth and by her desire to assert herself over someone weaker than she is.

Just as Priscilla stands as emotional slave to Zenobia, so Zenobia stands in bondage to Hollingsworth. His control over Zenobia also is demonstrated in the first scene they share. After Zenobia pulls back from Priscilla when Hollingsworth first brings her to Blithedale, Hollingsworth demands that Zenobia be kind and Zenobia acquiesces. Coverdale describes the exchange as follows: "But he [Hollingsworth] now looked stern and reproachful; and it was with that inauspicious meaning in his glance, that Hollingsworth first met Zenobia's eyes, and began his influence upon her life. To my surprise, Zenobia—of whose haughty spirit I had been told so many examples—absolutely changed color, and seemed mortified and confused" (pp. 28–29). At this point Coverdale does not know that Zenobia's attachment to Hollingsworth dates back seven years, so he is startled by the apparently immediate control Hollingsworth assumes. The control is demonstrated at greater length later at Eliot's pulpit, where the four major characters are gathered. Zenobia speaks eloquently on woman's rights, only to have Hollingsworth abruptly cut her off. The woman's role, he tells her, is "that of the sympathizer; the unreserved, unquestioning believer" of man. Again Zenobia volte-faces and agrees: " 'Well; be it so,' was all she said. 'I, at least, have deep cause to think you right. Let man be but manly and godlike, and woman is only too ready to become to him what you say!' " (p. 124). Then, after she goes off with Hollingsworth from the group, she falls to her knees before Hollingsworth, as Priscilla had done to her. In this position of the emotional slave she declares her love for Hollingsworth.

There is no doubt that Hollingsworth uses his control of Zenobia to his own advantage. Insofar as the furthering of his scheme to rehabilitate criminals is concerned, he is unscrupulous. He admits to Coverdale he hopes to buy Blithedale away from the brotherhood when it fails, as he is convinced it will, to convert it into his model reformatory. Thinking to use Coverdale's friendship, he tries to bring Coverdale into his plan. He fails with Coverdale, but succeeds with Zenobia. When Hollingsworth gives her up, she mentions the "disposition" she planned to make of her inheritance in his favor, without restriction. This certainly was the source of funds Hollingsworth had mentioned to Coverdale earlier when Hollingsworth tried to convince Coverdale his plan was feasible. Hollingsworth used Zenobia's love as a means toward obtaining money for his project. However, we cannot be sure of the extent to which he leads Zenobia on. We know he did not break off his relationship with Zenobia after she declared her love for him, and we know he did not stop the rumors about their future marriage. Yet, since he had not fallen in love with Priscilla at that stage, it is possible Hollingsworth was simply in the process of assessing his feelings for Zenobia. We know he helped Zenobia get

Priscilla away from Blithedale presumably to protect Zenobia's fortune, but, considering his shock at seeing Priscilla's performance in the theater, it is doubtful that he realized how much of a betrayal this was. In short, we see Hollingsworth taking advantage of his position of emotional master of Zenobia to gain access to money for his scheme, but we cannot be sure just how unscrupulous he is in his manipulations.

Zenobia thinks the worst of him. She charges him with raw, unabashed self-interest. Yet—and this is surely part of the ironic pattern of the book—the most serious prong of her attack could easily be turned back against her. She summarizes his offenses:

> First, you aimed a death-blow, and a treacherous one, at this scheme of a purer and higher life, which so many noble spirits had wrought out. Then, because Coverdale could not be quite your slave, you threw him ruthlessly away. And you took me, too, into your plan, as long as there was hope of my being available, and now fling me aside again, a broken tool! But, foremost, and blackest of your sins, you stifled down your inmost consciousness!—you did a deadly wrong to your own heart!—you were ready to sacrifice this girl, whom, if God ever visibly showed a purpose, He put into your charge, and through whom He was striving to redeem you! [p. 218].

A neat chronicle of Hollingsworth's sins, if he is seen from the worst angle. The first three sins—betrayal of the brotherhood, Coverdale, and Zenobia—are Hollingsworth's alone. But the fourth seems probably more valid against Zenobia, since it was her protection Priscilla originally sought. This Zenobia more or less admits at the conclusion of the accusation scene when she tells Priscilla, "You stood between me and an end which I desired. I wanted a clear path." Yet then she vacillates to the boast that she could have served Hollingsworth better "than the poor, pale flower he kept," Priscilla. Her insight into Hollingsworth's motives has brought her almost to an understanding of herself. She chokes it back as well as she can. Yet surely some understanding of herself remains to mingle with her sense of loss and to drive her toward suicide.

Behind these two master-slave relationships is a third, the rela-

tionship between Westervelt and Priscilla. The relationship is
mysterious and dark. It puts the master-slave predicament on a
level that is nearly archetypal. And surely critics Allan and Barbara Lefcowitz are not far wide of the mark—however reductive
their argument may be—when they find that Westervelt's control
of the girl exudes a certain musk of sexuality.[5] In this respect the
relationship parallels the sexuality between Hollingsworth and
Zenobia and perhaps even between Zenobia and Priscilla. This aspect is put before the reader by a member of the audience for
Priscilla's performance, who gossips about the power wizards such
as Westervelt have over the "will and passions" of others. The audience member recounts: "At the bidding of one of these wizards,
the maiden, with her lover's kiss still burning on her lips, would
turn from him with icy indifference; the newly made widow
would dig up her buried heart out of her young husband's grave,
before the sods had taken root upon it; a mother, with her babe's
milk in her bosom, would thrust away her child. Human character was but soft wax in his hands; and guilt, or virtue, only the
forms into which he should see fit to mould it" (p. 198). The wizard's power is absolute, and its context here is, in the main, sexual.
Immediately following this description of the wizard's power,
Westervelt enters with Priscilla. The remarks of the audience
member color our reaction to the relationship of Westervelt and
Priscilla and make the relationship seem sinister. This is not to say
that Westervelt has actually used Priscilla sexually. This is to suggest that he has the power to do so, if he chooses. Here probably
we are at the root of Priscilla's fear of her stage life and her desire to escape to Blithedale.

Certainly the relationship Westervelt describes to the audience
is one of complete control. "And yet, were I to will it," he tells
the audience about Priscilla, "sitting in this very hall, she could
hear the desert-wind sweeping over the sands, as far off as Arabia;

5 Allan and Barbara Lefcowitz, "Some Rents in the Veil: New Light on
  Priscilla and Zenobia in *The Blithedale Romance*," *Nineteenth-Century
  Fiction*, XXI (December, 1966), 270. My argument is that the sexual
  control the Lefcowitzes find is a part of a larger kind of power struggle
  for control in general.

the ice-bergs grinding one against the other, in the polar seas; the rustle of a leaf in an East Indian forest; the lowest whispered breath of the bashfullest maiden in the world, uttering the first confession of her love! Nor does there exist the moral inducement, apart from my own behest, that could persuade her to lift the silvery veil, or arise out of that chair!" (p. 202). He boasts control of Priscilla's mind and soul.

At this point Hollingsworth, who has been watching the performance, chooses to act on Priscilla's behalf. It may be that Hollingsworth has had a moment of self-awareness, for surely he could have seen a good deal of himself reflected in the way Westervelt was controlling and using another human being. Or it may be that Hollingsworth suddenly realized the extent of his feeling for Priscilla and wanted to free her from another's control. In either case, whatever Hollingsworth's self-knowledge, the result is the same. His reaction against the master-slave relationship of Westervelt and Priscilla brings him to make a sympathetic commitment to his "veiled lady." For him this is a complete reversal.

His act of sympathy for Priscilla, in its turn, ought to serve as a self-revealing moment for Zenobia. Hollingsworth has performed the action which Priscilla originally sought from Zenobia and which Zenobia was incapable of fulfilling. As we have noted, Zenobia partially admits her cruelty to Priscilla, but in her anguish she turns to attacks on the other characters and protects herself from deeper self-awareness. Nonetheless, we may assume that some increased awareness of what she has done to Priscilla, along with her despair at losing Hollingsworth and her desire to punish him for deserting her, drives her to suicide.

Here the chain of events stops. While we might expect the narrator to see the essential seriousness of the various relationships after he is forced to confront Zenobia's rigid corpse, and while we might expect him to go back and probe the motives of the characters involved in the chain of events leading to the suicide, we find, in fact, that the narrator does nothing. The memory of the discovery of the corpse stays with him; he resents the loss of his undeclared loved one, Priscilla; and he offers a glib appraisal of Hollingsworth's too strong devotion to a cause. But essentially Coverdale has gained no knowledge of human relationships from the rich material before him.

In Coverdale Hawthorne offers an alternative to the manipulators in the rest of the book. He presents Coverdale as the completely detached man. Not that Coverdale would not like to be a manipulator. He is just not capable of the involvement in life necessary for even the misuse of human sympathy. Hawthorne constantly mocks Coverdale by having him report foolish things with a straight face. An amusing instance of this is the scene when Coverdale pictures Brook Farm as a Garden of Eden and Zenobia as Eve. When Zenobia responds that she would prefer not to dress like Eve until the weather grows warmer, Coverdale becomes flustered by visions of Zenobia clad only in the proverbial fig leaf. His reaction is amusingly prudish, because he is obviously quite struck by Zenobia's "ample figure." In another instance he congratulates himself on catching a glimpse of Zenobia's white shoulder, only to moralize more discretionally in a following scene, "What was visible of her full bust—in a word, her womanliness incarnated—compelled me sometimes to close my eyes, as if it were not quite the privilege of modesty to gaze at her" (p. 44). Then, in his sickbed, he ponders whether or not Zenobia is a virgin, decides she is not, and finally chides himself for his prurient interest in the subject in the first place. Comically enough, Zenobia catches him in his meditation and asks him to stop his "eyeshot." All this would be quite acceptably amusing if Coverdale were a minor character in a Fielding comic novel, but he is not. He is the narrator of a chain of events leading to a suicide in Zenobia's case and a life of penance in Hollingsworth's case. The tragic elements clash with the comic narrator and produce irony.

Coverdale's hesitant spying is shown on a much more serious level when he moves back to Boston and uses his rear window as a vantage point for further peering around. At first he is merely the slightly absurd Paul Pry he was with Zenobia. From a safe distance he watches and even participates in the scenes of life of the dwellers behind him. Then, through a curtain analogous to the veil in the story of Theodore, Coverdale sees a girl he makes out to be Priscilla. Surprised and somewhat alarmed, he tries to unpuzzle the situation. Another window, uncurtained, reveals to him Zenobia and Westervelt in an excited conversation, presumably about Priscilla. Of course, maladroit as Coverdale is, he is caught again at his prying, and the curtain is dropped over the clear window. But Coverdale has seen enough to know that Zenobia and Westervelt are in collusion. Since he distrusts Westervelt and knows Zenobia's capacity for cruelty, Coverdale has every reason to be concerned for Priscilla's safety. His prying has brought him to the point where he is inextricably involved in the lives of the others, whether he likes it or not. It has brought him to the point where he must make a commitment to Priscilla, or by his very inaction he will be making a commitment to the plot of Zenobia and Westervelt. To give Coverdale what credit is his, we must admit that he does go to the apartment and demand to see Priscilla. Yet he allows Zenobia and Westervelt to take Priscilla away before he can find out what her situation is. Coverdale asks Priscilla if her choice is to go with Westervelt and Zenobia. But a gesture of "kind invitation" draws Priscilla to Westervelt, and she leaves on his arm without answering. In order to break the control Westervelt has on Priscilla, Coverdale needs to act more strongly. Hollingsworth's bold overthrow of Westervelt at the village hall proves that. Coverdale, however, is incapable of strong action, and so must stand an unwilling ally to Westervelt's and Zenobia's using of Priscilla. The title of the chapter in which Coverdale's confrontation takes place—"They Vanish"—suggests again the parallel between Coverdale and Theodore. Here Coverdale's "veiled lady" vanishes, because Coverdale would not commit himself to her.

The confrontation scene is indicative of Coverdale's action throughout the whole of the book. He gets a partial glimpse of a complex human situation, partially understands it, and partially acts on this understanding. In all phases he responds incompletely. His initial decision to come to Blithedale is made half in skepti-

cism and half in affirmation of the brotherhood. When Hollingsworth invites Coverdale into his scheme, Coverdale rejects Hollingsworth's treachery, but does not alert the brotherhood to Hollingsworth's plot. Coverdale stays in the middle. Similarly, after
leaving Blithedale for the first time, Coverdale says of his absorption with Zenobia, Priscilla, and Hollingsworth: "Together with
an inexpressible longing to know their fortunes, there was likewise a morbid resentment of my own pain, and a stubborn reluctance to come again within their sphere" (p. 194). He would
know their lives, but he would also stay invulnerable to the anguish that might arise from committing himself to any of them.
Returning to Blithedale from the city, he muses in the same vein,
"I laughed with the bitterness of self-scorn, remembering how unreservedly I had given up my heart and soul to interests that were
not mine. What had I ever had to do with them? And why, being
now free, should I take this thraldom on me, once again?" (p.
205). His statement about "unreservedly" giving himself up is dubious. Yet his question concerning his motives for putting himself
in a position where his reserve will be threatened is a good one.
The answer to his question is that he is fascinated with life, while
he is unable to accept its harshness and the demands of its ties.

He responds incompletely later when he tries to console Zenobia after Hollingsworth has left her. There is a partial bond between Coverdale and Zenobia, for he too has been forsaken by
Priscilla, albeit unknowingly on Priscilla's part. But Coverdale will
not speak of this. Formally he asks, "Can I do you any service?"
Zenobia gauges her answer exactly right. She tells Coverdale,
"You have really a heart and sympathies, as far as they go." Her
implication is that his heart and sympathies do not go far enough
to help her now. So she asks him to bear her message to Hollingsworth and her flower, symbol of her vitality, to Priscilla, and
leaves him. "Worn out with emotion on my own behalf and sympathy for others," Coverdale actually sleeps while Zenobia takes
her life.

Her suicide has no effect on him unless it be to frighten him
further from involvement in life. The memory of Zenobia's corpse

haunts him, he says. Yet it does not influence the course of his life. Comparing himself with Hollingsworth, Coverdale says, "I lack a purpose. How strange! He was ruined, morally, by an overplus of the very same ingredient, the want of which, I occasionally suspect, has rendered my own life all an emptiness" (p. 246). Zenobia's death brings him no nearer to understanding the need to enter the world of other human beings actively and sympathetically.

Perhaps Hawthorne's metaphor of the masquerade, one of his typical processions of life, best serves to clarify Coverdale's failing. On his return from Boston, Coverdale encounters the members of the brotherhood acting out a masquerade in the forest. The scene brings together much of the earlier imagery and action of the romance. In the first place, the masquerade culminates the imagery of the veils and window curtains which hide the identity of Priscilla. It also culminates the idea of the characters presenting an illusory exterior.[6] The bearded Westervelt with his false teeth is virtually all illusory surface. So too Hollingsworth and Zenobia, in their pretended roles in the brotherhood which they plan to convert to Hollingsworth's reformatory, present a false exterior. Most important, however, the masquerade sums up the theme of Coverdale's probing beneath the surface identities of Priscilla, Zenobia, and Hollingsworth. It sums up this theme in the sense that it expands the significance of Coverdale's probings to a more explicitly universal context.

At the masquerade, Coverdale looks upon the hurly-burly of life and sees beneath the surface. He sees an Indian in war paint, the goddess Diana with bow and a lazy hound, a Bavarian broomgirl, a Jim Crow, a Kentucky woodsman; these mingled with a quaint Shaker elder, shepherds from Arcadia, and allegorical figures of *The Faerie Queene*. Hawthorne emphasizes the bizarre-

6 A group of critics finds yet another purpose in the masquerade. They see it as a ritualistic fall festival which emphasizes nature's self-renewal as opposed to the lack of renewal of the inhabitants of Blithedale. The point is well taken, but it is not vitally relevant to my argument in this chapter. The most convincing critic in this "pastoral" school is Peter B. Murray, "Mythopoesis in *The Blithedale Romance*," PMLA, LXXV (December, 1960), 591–596.

ness of the mixture. As Coverdale watches the group from behind
a tree, it grows more and more strange until it becomes for him
almost a hallucination. First his tree is struck by an arrow from
the bow of the Diana. Then the revelers join in a furious dance.
Tam O'Shanter's fiend plays the music. Coverdale describes the
effect of the dance: "So they joined hands in a circle, whirling
round so swiftly, so madly, and so merrily, in time and tune with
the Satanic music, that their separate incongruities were blended
all together; and they became a kind of entanglement that went
nigh to turn one's brain, with merely looking at it" (p. 210). At
the dance's end, Coverdale's reaction is to laugh, partly as relief
and partly because he is "tickled by the oddity of surprising my
grave associates in this masquerading trim." Mock-seriously, the
dancers call the "profane intruder" to come forward to join their
procession of life. He flees them, going deep into the forest until
he stumbles over some logs piled and forgotten by a long-dead
woodman.

The episode works on two levels beyond the literal. First it
holds the brotherhood up as a group of masqueraders who may
be playing at the game of brotherhood just as they are playing
their game in the forest. However, second and much more important, the masquerade roles the characters assume and the dance
they do reveal their basic humanness more fully to Coverdale. He
is able to get beneath the grave exteriors they had presented up
until this time. He can see their emotional selves. The episode,
then, is a reworking of the story of the Veiled Lady and a reworking of much of what Coverdale has done earlier in the novel.
He looks beneath the surface of these people into their emotional
selves. The spectacle is both comic and frightening, and so Coverdale's reaction is to laugh derisively at the comic and flee from
the frightening aspect into isolation. He will not accept the spectacle of common humanness. His dilemma is Theodore's. He protects himself from all contact with the human self beneath the
veil.

Hawthorne concludes *The Blithedale Romance* by balancing
Coverdale against Hollingsworth. The one is incapable of human

ties, and the other uses human ties to further his selfish aims. Each
has been equally guilty of misusing life, at different extremes. Yet
of the two, Hollingsworth ends better. He has gained in self-
knowledge while Coverdale has not. As we have said, he learns of
the consequences of manipulating human lives when he sees Priscilla in the hands of Westervelt on the stage. From his knowledge
comes his love for Priscilla. Yet because of the ties that existed
between Zenobia and him, he cannot pursue his love for Priscilla
without greatly hurting Zenobia. Just how strong those ties were
and how great the hurt was are revealed to him in the suicide. He
must carry his guilt for this through the rest of his life. Yet at the
same time, his knowledge of himself and of human relations has
brought him to the point where he can form a sympathetic tie
with another human being. At the end of the novel he properly
knows the supreme value of his marriage to Priscilla. Coverdale,
the man who never entered life, need not blame himself so much
for Zenobia's suicide, but by the same token his life is void of any
regenerative tie. He has only his unspoken love to hold forever in
check.

The romance has puzzled readers for a long time. The reason
for this is that they have failed to grant Hawthorne the capacity
to put such richness of tone into the romance form. But *The
Blithedale Romance* does hold a careful fusion of the tragic Hawthorne with the comic Hawthorne, in irony. To achieve this fusion, as all post-Jamesian critics have noted, Hawthorne had to in-
vent the Jamesian narrator before James. Furthermore, he had to
reverse the normal process of tragi-comedy. While we easily accept tragedy that slips back into comedy, we find it difficult to
give up the detachment of comedy for the identification necessary in tragedy. Few authors, short of Shakespeare with Falstaff in
the *Henry IV* and *Henry V* history plays, can accomplish such a
reversal. Even modern novelists, with the benefit of a much more
sophisticated novel tradition to fall back on, prefer to make clear
on the first page the exact proportions of comedy and tragedy
they will use. Hawthorne sets up the distance of comedy, and then
through flashes of cruel manipulations brings the reader to the

stark, grim suicide. To appreciate this work, we need to realize he sets up the romance world, different, removed from our world, and then gradually breaks down the romance concept by bringing the action down into the meanest level of experience—three men dredging a river for a corpse with a hooked pole. The return to the grimness of the real world heightens our awareness of the artifice in the work and the author's presence as the manipulator of tone.

Chapter VI

The Marble Faun:
Hawthorne's romance
of the Adamic myth

The Marble Faun is a curiously modern book. Generally, critics have not recognized that fact and have tended to ask the wrong questions about the work and to express dissatisfaction with it for the wrong reasons. My contention is that *The Marble Faun* is Hawthorne's final experiment with methods of creating the artistic distance of romance and using artifice to probe self-consciously for meaning. In this work he interests himself singlemindedly with fabricating the substance and texture of archetypal myth. Surely we can all agree that the work is flawed. It is too prolix. Like the American tourist with his slide collection, Hawthorne has brought back too many recollections of Italy. But our basis for discussing its flaws ought to reside in our seeing it as an experiment with the presentation of myth. For Hawthorne *The Scarlet Letter* was a culminating effort with the form of the historical romance. In *The House of the Seven Gables* and *The Blithedale Romance* he turned to comedy and to irony as modes to work with. Now myth.

Hawthorne's kind of experimentation in *The Marble Faun* ought to be obvious to us, because it is exactly the kind of experimentation with artifice going on among modern, anti-realist writers. Consider, for example, the remarks of John Hawkes, author of *The Lime Twig* and *The Second Skin*, during a 1964 interview:

> My novels are not highly plotted, but certainly they are elaborately structured. I began to write fiction on the assumption that the true enemies of the novel were plot, character, setting, and theme, and having once abandoned these familiar ways of thinking about fiction, *totality of vision* or *structure* was really all that remained. And structure—*verbal and psychological coherence*—is still my largest concern as a writer. Related or corresponding event, recurring image and recurring action, these constitute the essential substance or meaningful density of my writing [italics mine].[1]

Hawkes claims accurately of his own work that he has stripped away concern with plot and character. So has Hawthorne. That characters of both are not "round" is irrelevant to the aims of both writers. And Hawthorne's conclusion added to the second edition of *The Marble Faun* makes clear that he, like the modern writer, has little interest in working out the details of plot. Hawthorne differs from Hawkes in his emphasis on setting and theme. Assuredly these are most important elements to Hawthorne. But they are important mainly as they contribute to what Hawkes calls "totality of vision" or the structure of "verbal and psychological coherence." Hawthorne's aim is to create a world of myth, related to our world but universal and separate. He draws heavily on "related or corresponding event, recurring image and recurring

1 Hawkes, "John Hawkes: An Interview," *Wisconsin Studies in Contemporary Literature*, VI (Summer, 1965), 149.

action" to make up the texture of that world. The use of setting, almost always symbolic as well as descriptive of the Italian scene, and the use of theme, in itself a kind of "recurring action" in *The Marble Faun*, contribute mightily to that world he makes. So it is the texture and meaning of the *total vision*, the mythic construct, we must examine.

The romance is an endless series of repetitions and balances.[2] Virtually every action and every symbolic object are reflected over and over as if caught in two facing mirrors. Each comes to us with a "sense of ponderous remembrances" demonstrably attached, or else it stands against a contrasting action or object. In other words, the progress of the book stems from association and contrast. These are properties we most often think of as operating in the flow of the subjective mind, particularly in a dream. Of course in modified form they are staples of all fiction. However, the point is that in *The Marble Faun* they do not appear in modified form; rather, they are the guiding principles of the work's coherence. Beside them character and plot count for very little. We should not be surprised to find Hawthorne dealing with a dreamlike texture. We have seen that he used the dream as a metaphor for the distance of the romance. And beyond that, in 1842, he expressed the desire to write a work that was totally dreamlike: "To write a dream, which shall resemble the real course of a dream, with all its inconsistency, its strange transformations, which are all taken as a matter of course, its eccentricities and aimlessness—with nevertheless a leading idea running through the whole. Up to this old age of the world, no such thing ever has been written." [3] This statement, written eighteen years before the publication of *The Marble Faun*, is perhaps the best gloss on its technique that Hawthorne could have given us. In this work we are aware of the artist's mind, or a general disembodied mind be-

---

2 Cf. Dorothy Waples, "Suggestions for Interpreting *The Marble Faun*," *American Literature*, XIII (November, 1941), 224–239. I partially follow Miss Waples' suggestion that Freud's theory of repetition-compulsion can aid us in understanding the texture of the work.

3 *The American Notebooks by Nathaniel Hawthorne*, ed. Randall Stewart (New Haven, 1932), p. 99.

hind the work, moving dreamlike toward the total vision of a myth.

The principles Hawthorne used to create the dreamlike texture, the principles of balance and repetition, are established at the outset through art objects.[4] The romance opens in the sculpture gallery in the Capitol at Rome with the four major characters engaged in a dispute over whether Donatello is a living replica of the Marble Faun attributed to Praxiteles. Through the comparison, Hawthorne at once puts Donatello into a pattern of symbols recurring through time. Donatello recalls an image from the Arcadian Age before the founding of Rome, and he recalls an image of a conception that occurred to the sculptor of the Greek-Roman Age in which the statue was made. Along with this sense of an image repeated through history comes the sense of counterpoint, established during the first paragraph, in the statue of the Human Soul "with its choice of Innocence or Evil close at hand, in the pretty figure of a child, clasping a dove to her bosom, but assaulted by a snake." As the book continues, each of the major characters has contrasting art objects associated with him.

Kenyon's masterpiece is his statue of Cleopatra. It is a masterpiece because in it Kenyon portrays rich and complex human emotions. Cleopatra is caught in repose—"between two pulse-throbs." Yet, as Hawthorne puts it, "such was the creature's latent energy and fierceness, she might spring upon you like a tigress, and stop the very breath that you were now drawing, midway in

4 Two recent critics have argued that the art objects do much more than set the scene: Paul Brodtkorb, Jr., "Art Allegory in *The Marble Faun*," *PMLA*, LXXVII (June, 1962), 254–267; and Frederick W. Turner, III, "Hawthorne and the Myth of Paradise," *Serif*, III (September, 1966), 9–12. Brodtkorb finds an art allegory in the work, with Hilda representing the spirit of art or art's ideality and timelessness. This concept of art is opposed to the timebound, existential world of fallen man, represented by Rome and by Miriam. Turner argues just the opposite. He finds that art as an embodiment of knowledge is an agent of Donatello's fall. Both of these critics can argue a strong case by excluding the evidence offered by the other. This fact should indicate that we need a reading of the function of the art objects large enough to include both the concepts of art as a kind of purity and art as a kind of human knowledge.

your throat." [5] The statue represents Kenyon's understanding, perhaps intuitive only, of human passion. Miriam is so moved by the statue and the understanding it represents in the sculptor that for a moment she feels Kenyon might be someone with whom she could share the secret of her past sin. A contrasting side of Kenyon's nature, however, is shown in the small, delicately sculptured marble hand he has done. It is modeled on Hilda's hand; and Kenyon keeps it, reverentially, in an ivory coffer. For him it is a symbol of Hilda's purity, which he worships. Just the opposite from his Cleopatra, the hand reveals in him a wish to see woman as a saintly being above the level of common humanity. That he should choose the hand as symbol for other-worldliness is ironic, for in the rest of the book the image of the hand appears over and over as a sign of brotherhood between fallible mortals or else as an instrument for committing an act of sin.[6] Yet for Kenyon, quite surely the sculptured hand represents the fragile purity of the dove maiden in her tower.

With Miriam we also encounter contrasting art objects. She has done a series of violent biblical sketches—Jael driving the nail through the temples of Sisera and Judith with the head of Holofernes. They involve the idea of a woman gaining brutal revenge on a man, and they involve scenes, Hawthorne states, "in which woman's hand was crimsoned by the stain." The recurring image of the hand serves to tighten the motif of the use of art objects. Quite the reverse of her biblical sketches, Miriam has also done drawings of domestic and common scenes—such as a wedded pair at the fireside—in a highly idealized manner to stress the charm of an innocent world. In these sketches, however, there always appears a figure separated from the innocent scene, a figure of sadness and isolation. If we interpret the figure to be the artist herself,

---

5 *The Marble Faun: or, The Romance of Monte Beni,* Centenary Edition, (Columbus, 1968), p. 126.

6 See, e.g., pp. 44, 97, 147, 166, 170, 173, 177, 199, 203, 204, 207, 246, 285, 313, 321, 362, 364, 423, 447, 448, and 461. Perhaps these two aspects are almost one and the same thing. Such seems to be the case with Georgiana's hand-shaped stain in "The Birthmark." It makes her less than perfect and connotes a longing for a sympathetic clasping.

then these sketches would represent a yearning for innocence in Miriam, who is separated from it by her stain of sin. Probably we can think of both her impulse toward attractive innocence and her impulse toward destructive vengeance as contained in a third art object, her self-portrait. Hawthorne describes the picture in terms of such a duality: "Gazing at this portrait, you saw what Rachael might have been, when Jacob deemed her worth the wooing seven years, and seven more; or perchance she might ripen to be what Judith was, when she vanquished Holofernes with her beauty, and slew him for too much adoring it" (p. 48). Donatello reacts first by admiring the beauty, then by noticing the sadness of the face.

Associated with Donatello, we encounter first the Marble Faun and then the alabaster skull. The comparison with the Faun points up his innocence. The comparison, however, is not altogether flattering. Donatello and the Faun appear innocent in the sense of being without knowledge of moral principle and without the kind of intelligence which morality implies. Both are attractive, but attractive as sensual, subhuman beings. Still, the comparison with a Faun grants Donatello an association with a kind of innocence and with a kind of deification. However, the alabaster skull, reputedly modeled on the skull of an ancestor who had committed a crime, sits before Donatello in his tower as a representation of his crime and of his mortality. In all respects, it contrasts with the image of the Marble Faun. Beyond these two art objects is a third, the bust Kenyon makes of Donatello and leaves only partially finished. This bust does not, like Miriam's self-portrait, hold together the two aspects of his character. Rather, it represents a third stage in his development resulting from the confluence of the two aspects of his character. "It is the Faun," says Hilda, "but advancing towards a state of higher development" (p. 380).

The first art object associated with Hilda is the Virgin's shrine which she tends. It stands at one of the angles of the battlements of the tower she lives in, and it consists of a lamp burning before the Virgin's image. In her "customary white robe," surrounded by the swirls of doves from their tower cote, Hilda is a votary of the purity of the shrine. On the other hand, Hilda is also associated with the portrait of Beatrice Cenci by Guido Reni which she is copying. The portrait involves "an unfathomable depth of sorrow." For Hilda, the sorrow in Beatrice's face results from a sinless fall from innocence. For Miriam, the sadness comes from Beatrice's knowledge that some of the evil of the Cenci family is hers. To both, however, Beatrice is a human being touched by a sense of sin. The copy of Beatrice comes into closer association with Hilda later in the book when an artist catches sight of a sadness in Hilda's face, paints her as "Innocence, dying of a Blood-stain!" (p. 330), and receives comment that he has used Guido Reni's Beatrice for his model.

In all four cases there is a consistent pattern of contrast. Kenyon's delicate marble hand, Miriam's sketches of familiar scenes, the Marble Faun associated with Donatello, and the Virgin's shrine associated with Hilda all connote purity and innocence. These are balanced against Kenyon's Cleopatra, Miriam's biblical sketches, the alabaster skull owned by Donatello, and Hilda's copy of Beatrice. This pattern of balance in the art objects is only the beginning of contrasts and associations that become labyrinthine before the work ends, as we shall see. But the pattern is fundamental for introducing us to the dreamlike coherence the work has. The characters merge into the art objects they create and own, or at least we could say they become inseparable from them. The result is the reduction of the characters toward the quality of art objects and the raising of the art objects toward the human level. The point where they meet is the level where the romance exists in its world of myth. What we have been examining has been Hawthorne's means of creating a dreamlike texture where mythic action can take place.

The texture is complicated by Hawthorne's use of repeated images and scenes, altered slightly each time they appear, but definitely setting up a cyclical rhythm of action that is surreal in its incessant regularity.

An obvious example is the lady at the fountain. She is most fully discussed in the legend from Donatello's ancestral past. The mar-

ble nymph on the fountain of Monte Beni is said to represent a
water nymph who once lived in the fountain and loved one of
Donatello's ancestors. The lover, however, committed a crime
and, in attempting to wash the blood from his hands in the waters
of the fountain, caused the nymph to vanish from his life after one
final reappearance with his blood staining her brow. Her disappearance signals his break with innocence. But the imagery is more
complex than that. "The nymph might have comforted him in sorrow," explains Donatello, "but could not cleanse his conscience of
a crime" (p. 246). He implies that the lover sought too much in
the nymph by seeking absolution rather than comfort and therefore forfeited all right to solace. This situation is used in trans-
muted form throughout the book, associated with Miriam. It appears first in the image of the fountain gushing from a naiad's urn
in the center of the court where Miriam lives. The effect here is
simply a visual foreshadowing of the image pattern. In the next instance we see Miriam kneeling subservient to the model, Antonio,
by the fountain on the Pincian Hill, closely resembling a sin-
stained fountain nymph. Then, at the Fountain of Trevi, Miriam's
shadow is flanked in the water by the shadows of the model and
of Donatello. The one portends destruction through guilt, and
the other possible safety through regenerative love, the two alternatives open to Donatello's ancestor when he approached the fountain with his blood-soaked hands. Finally, Miriam receives Donatello's pledge of love in front of the fountain at Perugia, and as
they depart together Miriam is called "a Nymph of grove or fountain." The image of the lady at the fountain thus recurs over and
over, altered each time but also recognizably similar.

The same may be said for the image of the dark or veiled, isolated figure. This image is begun with the legend of Memmius,
who haunted the catacomb of St. Calixtus, and immediately it is
picked up in the cloaked form of Antonio. Such a figure also appears in the sketches of Miriam, as we have noted. There we inferred the figure was Miriam herself. But whether or not she is
the figure in the sketches, she indisputably adopts that role at
the book's end when she kneels veiled and alone on the floor of the

Pantheon. This scene, in turn, evokes memory of an earlier scene where the spectral form of Antonio was observed doing penance, in isolation, before the black crosses of the Colosseum. And also in the same network of imagery we would have to consider the "figure in the dark robe" who watches Donatello in the wayside retreat on his way to Perugia. It is reasonable to assume again that the isolated character is Miriam, but there is no real need to force such a conclusion. The figure is merely a continuation of the image of isolation that originated in the legend of Memmius.

Another image that appears in several variations throughout the book is the figure with hands out in a gesture of beneficent sympathy. The most important representation of this image comes in the statue of Pope Julius III, who seems to bless the reunion of Miriam and Donatello taking place beneath him: "There was the majestic figure stretching out the hand of benediction over them, and bending down upon this guilty and repentant pair its visage of grand benignity" (p. 323). But this bronze pontiff is a kind of variation of the statue of Marcus Aurelius on the summit of the Capitoline Hill, which is described in similar terms: "He stretches forth his hand, with an air of grand beneficence and unlimited authority, as if uttering a decree from which no appeal was permissible, but in which the obedient subject would find his highest interests consulted; a command, that was in itself a benediction" (p. 166). Then at her confession scene, Hilda receives a similar blessing from the priest of St. Peter's: "But, as he stretched out his hands, at the same moment, in the act of benediction, Hilda knelt down and received the blessing with as devout a simplicity as any Catholic of them all" (p. 362). Hawthorne repeats and complicates the image when he has Miriam raise her arms in a similar gesture toward Hilda and Kenyon in the Pantheon. Her gesture is both a benediction and a warning to keep back: ". . . she looked towards the pair, and extended her hands with a gesture of benediction. . . . They suffered her to glide out of the portal, however, without a greeting; for those extended hands, even while they blessed, seemed to repel, as if Miriam stood on the other side of a fathomless abyss, and warned them from its verge" (p. 461).

As a gesture of repulse, Miriam's movement also repeats Hilda's repellent gesture when Miriam went to her after the murder of the model: ". . . she put forth her hands with an involuntary repellent gesture, so expressive, that Miriam at once felt a great chasm opening itself between them two" (p. 207). Thus, over and over Hawthorne presents the same image in the same language, slightly altered.

He uses the device on a smaller scale too. For instance, Guido Reni's "Archangel Michael" appears in one form as a sketch, in another as a painting, and in a third as a mosaic. There is no particular development to be traced from version to version. We are concerned first with the mystery of whether the demon's face in the picture resembles the model's and second with the effect of the scene recurring over and over.

The book is framed by two festivals which, as we have seen in the earlier chapters, are always important to what Hawthorne has to say. The festivals of *The Marble Faun* are no exceptions. As usual, they represent the hurly-burly of life among men. In the first, which takes place at the Villa Borghese during a feast day, Miriam and Donatello dance in a throng of people, re-creating·a Golden Age, until the challenging specter of the model appears before them vying with Donatello in the dance. His presence abruptly shatters the mood of carefree innocence Miriam and Donatello had achieved. For Miriam the scene is dreamlike, and, we may be tempted to add, archetypal. "In Miriam's remembrance, the scene had a character of fantasy. It was as if a company of satyrs, fauns, and nymphs, with Pan in the midst of them, had been disporting themselves in these venerable woods, only a moment ago; and now, in another moment, because some profane eye had looked at them too closely, or some intruder had cast a shadow on their mirth, the sylvan pageant had utterly disappeared" (p. 90). The first festival is a microcosm of a fall from innocence. Like a theme in a musical composition, once introduced, the scene recurs fragmentarily throughout the work and finally emerges again in an expanded and much more developed form near the conclusion. We see a group of youths and maidens racing and playing in the Colosseum; we learn that wandering musicians come to Monte Beni during the summer to hold dances on the lawn for the *contadini;* and we observe the reunion of Miriam and Donatello taking place amid the market-day crowd with its juggler and organ-grinder in Perugia. In the countryside beyond Rome, Miriam and Donatello approach Kenyon masquerading as *contadini.* These serve to keep the image of the festival in our minds. Then comes the final festival scene. In a thematic sense, it begins where the first festival ended. Hawthorne describes its beginning as "like a feverish dream." It is both surreal and comic as was the case of the conclusion of the first festival scene, with the insane dance of the model. Kenyon, the protagonist in the last festival scene, confronts a gigantic female masquerader who shoots him with a cloud of lime dust. He is challenged in a way similar to the way Donatello and Miriam were challenged by the apparition of the model. But the scene progresses and changes. Kenyon is again confronted, but this time by Hilda dressed as a white domino, on the balcony above, who throws a rose to him, in direct contrast to the shot of the gigantic woman. Beginning where the first festival ended—with a confrontation with a frightening challenge in the whirl of human life—the second festival moves to a scene of resolution beyond the challenge. For the moment, however, we are less concerned with the meaning of the festivals than with their texture. Overtly dreamlike, the festivals blend into each other. Characters shift roles. Kenyon replaces Miriam and Donatello as they recede into the background. But the scene itself expands and moves toward a resolution.

This is the sense we have with all of the recurring images we encounter in the work. An image moves toward a resolution or continues to make its presence felt throughout the work (as the "Archangel Michael" does), taking clear precedence over concerns of character or plot. These images emerge from the central theme of the work. As we have observed, the psychological principles of association and contrast govern their movements and give them coherence. The resulting texture is the texture of a dream, where rational principles of organization cede to psychological principles. But more than that, the repetitiousness of the images and their patterns convinces us that we are engaged with a truth that occurs over and over, infinitely. We are convinced, in other words, that we are engaged with an archetypal experience, or experience on the level of myth. That the archetype shifts, Proteus-like, from image to image may bewilder us. But the process of locating it among its various shapes is a necessary one, for it is Hawthorne's equivalent to the suspense of plot and action in a more realistic novel. The excitement generated in *The Marble Faun* is analogous to the excitement generated in much of modern expressive literature, such as T. S. Eliot's *The Waste Land*, and even a modern film such as Robbe-Grillet's *Last Year at Marienbad*. The excitement consists in the reader's effort to pierce through shifting images to the constants beneath their changing surfaces. With these thoughts in mind, we may now look into the book's central theme and pursue the meaning of the work. The method of the book, we will find, is closely related to its meaning.

As several critics have noted, the central theme is the Adamic fall and consequent rise of mortal man.[7] Donatello is the most obvious embodiment of the archetype. His fall and rise form the thematic center of the book. Typically, his fall is foreshadowed before it actually takes place and then re-echoed after its occur-

7 Any treatment of the theme of the fall must begin with an acknowledgment of its indebtedness to Merle E. Brown's essay, "The Structure of *The Marble Faun*," *American Literature*, XXVIII (November, 1956), 302–313. Brown makes the point that all four of the main characters undergo falls and subsequent rises. The most articulate attacker of the idea of the fortunate fall is Hyatt H. Waggoner, "*The Marble Faun*," *Hawthorne: A Critical Study* (Cambridge, Mass., 1955), pp. 195–222. He argues that the fortunate fall entails a kind of Antinomianism which Hawthorne would not have accepted. Undoubtedly he is correct in this. But two other critics, Bernard J. Paris, "Optimism and Pessimism in *The Marble Faun*," *Boston University Studies in English*, II (Summer, 1956), 95–112, and Peter Beidler, "The Fortunate Fall in *The Marble Faun*," *Emerson Society Quarterly*, XLVII (1967), 56–62, have demonstrated that the fall raises a series of separable questions, some of which can be positively answered and some negatively. They show there are *some* fortunate consequences.

rence. It is foreshadowed in the garden of the Villa Borghese when Donatello wishes to kill the model because of the hold Antonio has on Miriam, and it is re-echoed in the legend of Donatello's ancestor who lost the fountain maiden through his crime. The actual fall, however, takes place when Donatello, at the bidding of Miriam, hurls the model from the Tarpeian Rock to his death. Donatello's first response after the crime is to feel drawn to Miriam in the complicity of the act. "So intimate, in those first moments," says Hawthorne, "was the union, that it seemed as if their new sympathy annihilated all other ties, and that they were released from the chain of humanity; a new sphere, a special law, had been created for them alone" (p. 174). The feeling disappears for Donatello when he realizes that the tie consists in guilt for their crime. He loses his innocence, but—precisely like Arthur Dimmesdale—is not able to accept his capacity to sin.

At Monte Beni, Donatello repents his sin and prepares to begin a new relationship with Miriam with the help of Kenyon. When Donatello meets Miriam at Perugia, he can begin a relationship of mutual consolation with her because he has come to accept the capacity to sin as a part of his nature and for that matter as a part of Miriam's. The tie between them now is quite different. It is a tie of mutual support and sympathy, but not the kind of tie that can guarantee an earthly happiness, since it is founded on an understanding of a capacity that both wish to purge from their characters. Kenyon puts it this way:

> ... your bond is twined with such black threads, that you must never look upon it as identical with the ties that unite other loving souls. It is for mutual support; it is for one another's final good; it is for effort, for sacrifice, but not for earthly happiness! ... Not, for earthly bliss, therefore, ... but for mutual elevation and encouragement towards a severe and painful life, you take each other's hands. And if, out of toil, sacrifice, prayer, penitence, and earnest effort towards right things, there comes, at length, a sombre and thoughtful happiness, taste it, and thank Heaven! [p. 322].

From this point on we can consider Donatello renewed. When we see him again, he is prepared to turn himself in to the authorities and submit to social law. More important, Miriam testifies that they have achieved the kind of "sombre and thoughtful happiness" Kenyon had spoken of. Concerning Donatello, she says: "He has travelled in a circle, as all things heavenly and earthly do, and now comes back to his original self, with an inestimable treasure of improvement won from an experience of pain" (p. 434).[8] Another way to see his development is in terms of Thorwaldsen's threefold analogy of the development of a statue which Kenyon expounds: "the Clay-model, the Life; the Plaister-cast, the Death; and the sculptured Marble, the Resurrection" (p. 380).[9] Or we can see Donatello's stages of development paralleled by three art objects: his innocence, the Marble Faun; his agony and education in his remorse, the bust of him that Kenyon makes and revises; and his renewal, the statue of Venus he discovers in the excavation, reassembles, and then leaves as a legacy to Kenyon. As usual, there is a long line of parallels to his movement. By the standards of the realistic novel, Donatello's change is unsuccessful, for much of the burden of detailing his change is borne by images rather than by directly presented action. But in Hawthorne's dreamlike nexus, an image is as dramatically valid as an action.

Miriam and Kenyon find the change in Donatello so striking that both turn their thoughts to the doctrine of the fortunate fall. First, Miriam suggests it to Kenyon, who tells her that she pushes her speculation beyond what she can know. Yet the idea apparently intrigues Kenyon, for later he whimsically suggests the doctrine to Hilda, who rejects it as he did before. The doctrine has seemed vitally important to more than several critics. Yet Hawthorne's reason for introducing it is probably to have it rejected and thereby to set the limits of what can be known about the archetypal situation he treats. Whether Donatello is better for

8 This is similar to the idea Holgrave expresses to Phoebe in *The House of the Seven Gables* when he speaks of a "second youth" attained through love. See *The House of the Seven Gables*, Centenary Edition, (Columbus, 1965), p. 215.
9 Cf. Roy Male, "The Transfiguration of Figures: *The Marble Faun*," *Hawthorne's Tragic Vision* (Austin, Tex., 1957), pp. 157-177. Male takes the threefold analogy to be the central metaphor of the work.

having fallen and having renewed himself than he would have been had he stayed innocent is essentially an unanswerable question. And it is a question that does not need to be answered. For Hawthorne man has fallen; man does have the capacity to sin in his nature; and in treating the human condition as he views it, Hawthorne does not need to go beyond those postulates. Perfectly adequate is the alternative which Miriam says Hilda would give: "... that Sin—which Man chose instead of Good—has been so beneficently handled by Omniscience and Omnipotence, that, whereas our dark Enemy sought to destroy us by it, it has really become an instrument most effective in the education of intellect and soul" (p. 435). And perfectly adequate is Kenyon's frank admission that the theological workings of the situation are unknown to him. What most of the characters—Miriam, Hilda, and Kenyon —recognize is that Donatello has advanced out of his debilitating sense of guilt.

Donatello's development contrasts with the development of the model. The model first appears against the background of Memmius, as Donatello did against the background of the Faun, and the model wears clothes of animal skin—a cloak of buffalo hide and breeches of goatskin—so that he looks like an "antique Satyr," an equivalent to the Faun Donatello resembles. As we have already observed, the two rivals mirror each other when they dance at the Villa Borghese and when they flank Miriam by the Fountain of Trevi. Yet more important, their relationships with Miriam are strangely similar up to the point of the final outcomes. From what we can determine of Miriam's past, the model was involved in a crime with Miriam, much as Donatello comes to be. In the confrontation after the festival at the Villa Borghese, Miriam says to the model, "Do you imagine me a murderess? ... You, at least, have no right to think me so!" He answers, "Yet ... men have said, that this white hand [Miriam's] had once a crimson stain." And she responds, "It had no stain ... until you grasped it in your own!" (p. 97). Obliquely, they are talking about a crime that seems to have stained the model, leaving Miriam not legally guilty but somehow implicated. We know that Miriam had earlier broken a betrothal to a marchese of a branch of her paternal house, and we know the marchese had a strange "subtlety" of thin-blooded insanity. It would be reasonable to assume the crime had something to do with protecting Miriam against the marchese. This is suggested by Hawthorne's juxtaposition of the information about the broken betrothal with his reference to the "terrible event" in which Miriam was suspected "of being at least an accomplice." Yet this is only suggested, not pinned down. What we do know surely is that Antonio joined the Capuchins to do penance, just as Donatello was to retire to Monte Beni, and on refinding Miriam, as Donatello was to do, the model recognized a bond between Miriam and himself. Both men, then, enact the fall, but the model perishes whereas Donatello renews himself.

We must not press for too many motivational reasons why their outcomes differ, for Hawthorne is first and foremost using them to illustrate alternative possibilities of the fall. The fact that their outcomes do differ is the important thing for Hawthorne's design. But we may also note two divergences in their developments. First, the process of remorse drives the model insane, while Donatello has the good fortune to be led out of his remorseful isolation by Kenyon, who wisely tells him, "It was needful for you to pass through that dark valley, but it is infinitely dangerous to linger there too long" (p. 273). Second, the nature of the bond between the model and Miriam differs drastically from the bond between Donatello and Miriam in terms of control and freedom. The model uses his knowledge of their common sin to subjugate Miriam. But Miriam, in turn, refuses to allow factors of control to enter into her bond with Donatello. She withdraws when she recognizes her presence repels Donatello, and she insists she will not return to him until he wishes her to. When Kenyon offers to lead her to Donatello at the fountain of Perugia, Miriam responds: "No, Kenyon, no! . . . Unless, of his own accord, he speaks my name—unless he bids me stay—no words shall ever pass between him and me" (p. 317).

Another alternative possibility of the fall is represented by the developments of Kenyon and Hilda. Both of them try to cling to the idea of Hilda's innocence, despite the knowledge of man's capacity to sin which is forced on them. From the beginning of the work, however, we know they have the latent ability to understand sin. If Hilda had not such a latent ability, she could not have duplicated Guido Reni's process of creating Beatrice Cenci, and Kenyon, without such an ability, could not have created his Cleopatra.

After Hilda has witnessed the murder, she puts off Miriam's attempt to elicit sympathy out of fear of the consequences. She says: "If I were one of God's angels, with a nature incapable of stain, and garments that never could be spotted, I would keep ever at your side, and try to lead you upward. But I am a poor, lonely girl, whom God has set here in an evil world, and given her only a white robe, and bid her wear it back to Him, as white as when she put it on. Your powerful magnetism would be too much for me. The pure, white atmosphere, in which I try to discern what things are good and true, would be discoloured" (p. 208). Hilda may have no clear conception of what sin is, as Miriam tells her at the end of this speech, but Hilda's statement shows that she is aware of her capacity to sin. Instead of this knowledge giving her a basis of sympathy for Miriam, it fills her with fear that she will be corrupted and her narrow, moral absolutes overturned. Hence she pulls back into isolation, as Donatello and the model had done. After a time she is able to move out of her isolation toward an affirmation of the human condition. The movement is slow. It begins with her confession to the Catholic priest, an act of communication when she can bear isolation no longer. It continues with her more open relationship with Kenyon that comes after the relief of the confession. He educates her to the complexity of Miriam and Donatello's relationship: "Worthy of Death, but not unworthy of Love!" Gradually she comes to a fuller understanding: "It was not that the deed looked less wicked and terrible, in the retrospect; but she asked herself whether there were not other questions to be considered, aside from that single one of Miriam's guilt or innocence; as, for example, whether a close bond of friendship, in which we once voluntarily engage, ought to be severed on

account of any unworthiness, which we subsequently detect in
our friend. For, in these unions of hearts, (call them marriage, or
whatever else,) we take each other for better, for worse" (p. 385).
This passage is a complete reversal of the self-interest seen in the
above speech Hilda made to Miriam. Having come to this larger
understanding of the need to affirm one's ties with other fallible
mortals, Hilda is ready to undertake her errand to Miriam's family, an act symbolic of Hilda's affirmation.

Kenyon follows the same course on a much less intense level.
He rebuffs Miriam by his manner when she tries to confess her
past sin to him. Only after he has been gradually drawn into
Donatello's anguish and has his sympathy awakened for his friend
is Kenyon ready to hear Miriam's confession. Even then, however, Kenyon keeps a nostalgic longing for innocence alive in himself through continuing to think of Hilda as a symbol of unblem-
ished purity. It gives him comfort and assurance to think of her in
terms of such a fixed moral quantity. But after he educates Hilda
to the complexity of the crime, she in turn educates him to the
complexity in herself. This she does through her act of involvement for Miriam. Certainly the act was more demanding than she
thought when she first went to the Cenci palace. Yet when her in-
ternment ended, she was satisfied to have served her friend even
to the extent of imprisonment. This is the new Hilda that Kenyon
may now cease to idolize as a priestess and may marry as a woman.

Thus, at the end of the work we are presented with three alternative possibilities of the fall. The model is destroyed. Donatello
and Miriam find a bond of sympathy, but because of the extent
that they were involved in the crime, are unable to live together
happily as man and wife. Kenyon and Hilda, through their involvement with the crime at a relative distance, survive well. The
crime brings them to a broader understanding of the human condition and makes it possible for them to love each other. As usual
in Hawthorne's works, *The Marble Faun* ends with a balance of
alternatives. Hawthorne's way is not to teach answers as much as
it is to demonstrate the complex predicament of the procession of
life.

The Marble Faun is about the myth of man's fall from innocence. In a way it is the story of Dimmesdale and Hester retold.
But retold quite differently. It consists almost entirely of its surface
texture. An image blends into another, moves to an opposite, and
blends anew into another image. The characters are barely distinguished from the art objects around them; both essentially serve
as images carrying meaning. All this may be perplexing to us if we
approach *The Marble Faun* with the idea of probing deeply into
the psychological motivation of the characters. But that is only
one way to approach literature. We would not seek to probe
deeply into Eliot's Belladonna in *The Waste Land.* We accept her
as a part of the over-all structure of the work and assign her no existence outside the work. We do not ask *why* she is afraid of the
sound outside her door; we accept her as a woman who *is* afraid
of the sound outside her door and ask how that role fits into the
rest of the work's structure. So it is with modern expressionistic
novels such as John Hawkes's *Lime Twig.* There again we do not
ask why Michael Banks dreams of a phantom horse which will destroy him. We accept him as one who dreams such a dream and
ask how his dream orders the structure and meaning of the whole
work. So too with Hawthorne. His subject is not four characters.
It is the myth of the fall. The characters only play roles in the depiction of that myth.

   To suggest *The Marble Faun* exists only on a surface level, of
course, is not to suggest the work is superficial. Far from it. The
surface of *The Marble Faun* is an extremely intricate and beauti-
fully wrought dream nexus. There are problems with the structure of the work, however. We can divide it into three sections.
The first Roman section (Chapters 1–23) mainly concerns Miriam
—her sin in the past, her relationship with Donatello, her attempts
to confide in Kenyon and Hilda, and the murder. The Monte Beni
section (Chapters 24–35) largely deals with Donatello's growing
awareness of the human condition. And the second Roman section (Chapters 36–50) centers on the educations of Hilda and Kenyon. The real subject matter comes, then, in Sections II and III,
where we see the effects of the crime. However, Section I bulks

almost as large as those two sections put together. Hawthorne apparently forgot his success in *The Scarlet Letter* when he began with the fall already an accomplished fact. In *The Marble Faun* he simply takes too long to get to the fall. Then, as we complained at the outset, there are just too many art objects. The device is kept up too long. Yet when we finish registering such complaints, we return inescapably to the fact that *The Marble Faun* is a dazzling piece of experimentation with the shifting surfaces of a mythic dream. The world Hawthorne creates in *The Marble Faun* is unique for its time. It is a work given coherence by a subjective, dreaming mind. It depends for its success on our accepting the process of this mind, as it turns and gropes toward realization of the Adamic myth, as the main strength of the work.

Conclusion

Hawthorne's four major works mark stages of experimentation with the form of the romance. In *The Scarlet Letter* he follows the three balances of romance scrupulously. The distance to the past is carefully set at the beginning and maintained throughout the work. The events seen as marvelous by the townspeople further help to establish distance between the reader's world and the world of romance. But the ideal patterns, the conceptualizations of human experience, are probably the work's most important formal aspect. Hawthorne establishes the boundaries for his human action by the conceptions of society and nature, the black Puritan and the fair Puritan, in the opening chapters. From this point on, he probes into the psyches of his characters and examines the positive and negative aspects of the antithetical poles he has established. But always we are aware of the work's boundaries. Everything outside the dilemma of the sinners has been cut away. Yet inside the work's boundaries, Hawthorne pursues a rich complex of alternatives evolving from his characters' discovery of sin in the human condition. We quickly become aware that Hawthorne is using his characters to explore quite self-consciously a range of possible consequences of the discovery. Dimmesdale, through humble acceptance of his capacity to sin and prideful rejection of its possibilities to degrade him, achieves the nearest equivalent to Grace which Hawthorne will grant—the release of transcendent death. Hester, lacking Dimmesdale's power to see beneath social consequences to ethical and moral universalities, continues as a lifelong penitent acting out a role society gives her, but a role which she can never fully understand. And Chillingworth, the opposite of Dimmesdale, achieves a fiendish balance of knowledge and pride which isolates him from men and destroys him. Thus we probe human experience in its diversity. But the diversity is circumscribed. Hawthorne explores it only within established boundaries. The result is a work of excruciating intensity. *The Scarlet Letter* succeeds because Hawthorne uses the distance of romance not as a means to escape life but as a means to make it more sharply focused. He realizes the claims of romance theory.

This accomplished, he experiments more and more with romance form. While the view of life in *The Scarlet Letter* is essentially tragic, Hawthorne turns to a consideration of more optimistic possibilities in *The House of the Seven Gables*. The central problem of ancestors' guilt from the past bearing on present generations, like the conflict of the fair Puritan and the black Puritan, is a standard romance situation. Hawthorne chooses to present the theme of expiation of the past guilt through a regenerative human evolution which parallels the regenerative cycle of nature. But while he presents his theme straightforwardly, he also mocks and parodies it in the characters of Hepzibah and Clifford. They are hopelessly weak examples of Pyncheon pride and appetite, and they are straw reproductions of the young lovers whose marriage erases the evil of the past. Thus Hawthorne uses the conscious artifice of romance distance to "debate" his comedic solution. At the same time, he continues to use the standard balances of the romance form. He ranges back and forth through history. He uses the marvelous aura of the curse, the mesmerism, and the ghosts of the Pyncheon mirror, lightly, to create the artificial world of the romance. And as we have noted above, the cycle of nature forms a kind of ideal pattern in which the human action takes place. But the primary piece of experimentation here is Hawthorne's use of Clifford and Hepzibah to call attention to the conscious artifice of the work. Suspended and charmed in the artifice of this world, we can accept the possibility of regeneration as an unalterable absolute.

In *The Blithedale Romance* Hawthorne continues to experiment with the romance form. The tone of his work is sharply ironic. The action comes to us through a disengaged narrator who misses the significance of what he tells us. Behind him, however, we can see a series of master and slave relationships which take place at the Blithedale community. History is not a factor in this work. The romance distance depends mainly on the unusualness of the Blithedale society. The mysterious Zenobia and the wizard Westervelt, exaggerated in the narrator's imagination, reinforce the unusualness of the community. While there are no "boundaries" as there were in *The Scarlet Letter*, the romance is almost as highly patterned. Parallel master and slave relationships and repetition of the situation of inquiring into the secret life of characters give the work its highly ordered structure.

The Marble Faun is far and away Hawthorne's most ambitious extension of romance form. Stages of history, marvelous events and characters, the ideal pattern of the fall of man, all compress themselves into Hawthorne's mythic or dream fabric. Hawthorne calls our attention to his artifice here through his use of the art objects. The human world and the world of artifice blend into each other. The guiding principles of the romance are the psychological ones of association and contrast. Scenes lead to other scenes according to those principles. Linear plot becomes relatively unimportant. The totality of effect of the dream world, held at a distance from the real world, not too close, not too far, is Hawthorne's aim. It is the aim of romance theory, but that aim treated as no other writer of the era could conceive of trying. Hawthorne re-creates the process of a disengaged mind working out the Adamic myth in a series of variations.

Running through all four of these romances is the central dilemma of characters cut off from the main body of mortal men. In each work they must affirm sympathetic ties with the "procession of life," for that is the only sphere in which Hawthorne considers life real. Romantic individualism, for Hawthorne, is a deception—an interesting one perhaps, but still a deception. Hawthorne does not vary his attitude toward the importance of this dilemma. He attacks it from different angles, and he considers differing possibilities of the dilemma, but always it is there at the center of his work. Because he was so clear on the nature of his central dilemma, if not its solution, he could devote a large measure of his creative energy to the development of form.

I have traced a progression of experimentation with form beginning with *The Scarlet Letter* and ending with *The Marble Faun*. The progression does not imply "improvement," for surely all readers agree *The Scarlet Letter* is Hawthorne's masterpiece. It does show, however, the devotion to craft of the artist engaged in finding out the possibilities of his fictional method. It is this kind of devotion to craft that allowed Hawthorne to write *The Scarlet Letter* in the first place, and it is this kind of devotion that produced the other important advances in form we have looked at. Beginning with the raw materials of his era, Hawthorne moved to an astounding formal sophistication.

Toward the end of his career, Hawthorne tried and failed to write four more romances.[1] The nature of his failures is instruc-

1 Edward Davidson has studied these unfinished romances at length. I have drawn on the following of his works: *Hawthorne's Last Phase*

tive. These romances fall into two groups: romances of the search
for an ancestral heritage in England and romances concerning the
search for an elixir of life. The first group began with the draft
called *The Ancestral Footstep* in 1858, before Hawthorne wrote
The Marble Faun, and continued with the various versions of
Doctor Grimshawe's Secret, which Hawthorne struggled with
from June of 1860 to the spring of 1861. The second group consists of the various manuscript materials relating to *Septimius Felton*, which he worked on from 1861 to 1863, and the chapters of
The Dolliver Romance, which he wanted to prepare in 1863 and
1864 for serial publication in *The Atlantic Monthly*. The "English" romance involves a young English orphan brought to America by a mysterious doctor, who raises him along with a young
girl and plays out hints and taunts about the boy's background in
England. After the doctor's death, the young man journeys to
England to inquire into his past. Wounded by assailants, he is taken
to a small charity hospital where he is cared for by the warden
and a pensioner, both of whom resemble the doctor who raised
him. He encounters a girl who appears to be the one he grew up
with. And eventually he confronts an Italian nobleman in control
of what might be the hero's estate. The Italian is an ancestral double whom the hero must somehow defeat or lay to rest. The
"elixir" romance also alludes to the theme of a mysterious ances-
try, but mainly concerns the search to unravel a previously discovered secret concoction that will give everlasting life. *Septimius Felton* takes place during the Revolutionary War. The hero
kills a British soldier who may also be an ancestral double to the
hero and obtains the mysterious formula from him. He elects to
pursue the mystery of the formula. The fragments of *The Dolliver Romance* deal with an aged apothecary who apparently has
the elixir in his possession and must determine how to use it.

Leaving aside the question of Hawthorne's weak health in his
last years, we can see that these works fail for two primary rea-

(New Haven, 1949); *Hawthorne's Doctor Grimshawe's Secret* (Cambridge, Mass., 1954); and "The Unfinished Romances," *Hawthorne Centenary Essays* (Columbus, 1964), pp. 141–163.

sons. In the first place, Hawthorne has lost his sure sense of the moral dilemma which he wants to treat. In the inquiry into the past inheritance of the "English" romance, Hawthorne is not sure of his hero's motives and he is not sure what the heritage should be. At times we find Hawthorne edging toward the idea of a past guilt to be expiated. But for him to write a romance on such a theme would be to repeat *The House of the Seven Gables*. In *Septimius Felton* the idea of the elixir serving to break the hero's ties with the human condition interests Hawthorne. This seems to be the theme he settles on at the end when the hero's loved one uses the so-called elixir to poison herself. But here again Hawthorne seems merely on the verge of repeating a theme he had handled successfully in the past in stories like "The Birthmark" and "Rappaccini's Daughter." The unfinished romances are not bankrupt of ideas, however. The situations of the mysterious doubles in the Italian nobleman and the Revolutionary War soldier are rich with possibilities. True, Hawthorne did touch on this in the opposition of Donatello and the model in *The Marble Faun*, but we could hardly say he gave the idea of the double full treatment. Why does Hawthorne not recognize this opposition as a possible focus for his romances? The answer may be that it would carry him further away from the dilemma of the individual and the "procession of life" than he chooses to go. In any case, we may conclude that his attempts to work the subjects of the ancestral inheritance and the elixir of life around to a statement on that dilemma did not succeed and that he did not, or was not willing, to go on to a different kind of moral conflict.

In the second place, Hawthorne was unable to find the kind of experimental form he apparently needed to stimulate him. *The Marble Faun* seems to have exhausted his capacity to push the romance form further. A simple use of a foreign land as a source of romance distance, a real possibility to him when he wrote *The Ancestral Footstep*, could hardly have been appealing to him after his extensive use of the Italian setting. There of course remained open to him the possibility of writing a novel of manners on the clash of the American and European of the kind that Henry

James was to perfect. Certainly this was one of his intentions in *Doctor Grimshawe's Secret*. But Hawthorne was unable to do this. His mind turned too often to the abstracting process of the romancer. Seen in this light, the return to historical distance and extensive use of the marvelous in *Septimius Felton* marks a retreat to the staples of the conventional romance and indicates Hawthorne's inability to go further with experimentation. His notes to himself in the manuscript margins indicate that he knew quite well he was retreating to conventionalities. But while this knowledge was enough to cause him to break off his work time and time again, it could not help him reverse his course. In *The Marble Faun* he exhausted his capacity to create new forms.

The lesson of the failures is instructive because it directs us to the roots of Hawthorne's strength. Primarily he was a creator of forms and textures. Having arrived at a moral dilemma that he could be sure was overwhelmingly important, he was free to experiment with modes for treating the dilemma. He depended both on his sureness of the central conflict and on the stimulation of experimentation with form. Without these he could not go on. The romance theory which he assimilated from the unrealized claims of his contemporaries was uniquely suited to his interest in form. This theory makes the act of creating order one of the highest possible literary acts. Sure of his thematic nexus in his four major romances, Hawthorne devoted himself to the pursuit of form as the means of making life intelligible.

Index

Allegory: considered part of romance form, xii; abstract quality, 50; in "Young Goodman Brown," 71; not descriptive of *The Scarlet Letter*, 82

Ambiguity: considered Hawthorne's forte, x; structured, xi, 81; inadequate term *per se*, 7

Aristotle, 28

Artifice: Hawthorne's emphasis on, xiv–xv, 3, 6–7; in *The Marble Faun*, 27, 139, 160; in "Main Street," 50; Hawthorne's self-consciousness, 50–51; in "The Artist of the Beautiful," 53–60; in "Rappaccini's Daughter," 60–65; in structure of black and fair Puritans, 85, 100; in *The House of the Seven Gables*, 103, 116–119, 160; in *The Blithedale Romance*, 122, 137

Barker, Benjamin: *The Gold Hunters*, 16

Bridge, Horatio, 101

marvelous, 25–26; as detached narrator, 121–122, 130–135; compared to Theodore, 123; balanced against Hollingsworth, 135–136

Dimmesdale, Arthur: as complex hero, 85–92; pride, 92–96; his role compared to Hester's, 98–100; his role compared to Chillingworth's, 100

Donatello: as marvelous faun and natural man, 21, 26; linked with art objects, 143; legend of ancestral past, 144–145; as dancer in procession of life, 147; Adamic figure, 149–152; contrasted to the model, 152–153

Guasconti, Giovanni, 60–65

Hilda: linked with art objects, 143–144; role in the Adamic myth, 153–155

Holgrave: as romantic lover, 109–112, 114; as teller of the story-within-the-story, 116–117

Hollingsworth: his master-slave relationship with Zenobia, 126–128; balanced against Coverdale, 135–136

Kenyon: linked with art objects, 141–142; as protagonist in the procession of life, 148; role in the Adamic myth, 153, 155

Miriam: linked with art objects, 142–143; as woman of the fountain, 145; as supplicant, 145–146

Molineux, Robin, 67–71

Prynne, Hester: as fair Puritan, 84–85; attempt to adjust to society's classification of her, 96–100; her role compared to Dimmesdale's, 98–100

Prynne, Pearl: supernatural dimensions, 21, 23; her effect on Dimmesdale, 89–91; her effect on Hester, 97–98

Pyncheon, Clifford: as a character of parody, 105, 108–109, 112–114

Pyncheon, Hepzibah: as a character of parody, 105, 107–108, 112–114

Pyncheon, Jaffrey, 105, 107, 109, 117–118

Pyncheon, Phoebe: as romantic lover, 109–112, 114

Rappaccini: as controller, 61–62, 64–65

Rappaccini, Beatrice: as natural purity, 62–65

Warland, Owen, 53–60

Zenobia: on the marvelous, 25–26; her story-within-the-story, 123–124; her master-slave relationship with Priscilla, 124–126; her master-slave relationship with Hollingsworth, 126–128

—Romances:

The Ancestral Footstep, 162–164

The Blithedale Romance: irony with moral purpose, 18–19; the marvelous, 25–26; irony, 120–122, 136–137; Coverdale as detached narrator, 121–122, 130–135; the story-within-the-story, 122–124; Zenobia's master-slave relationship with Priscilla, 124–126; Hollingsworth's master-slave relationship with Zenobia, 126–128; Westervelt's master-slave relationship with Priscilla, 128–130; the procession of life, 134–135; balance of Coverdale and Hollingsworth, 135–136; as experimentation with form, 160

A Note on the Author

John Caldwell Stubbs is assistant professor of English at the University of Illinois. He received his B.A., magna cum laude, from Yale University in 1958, and his Ph.D. from Princeton University in 1963. He has published several articles in literary journals. *The Pursuit of Form: A Study of Hawthorne and the Romance* is his first book.

UNIVERSITY OF ILLINOIS PRESS